Flight from London to Berlin

Jacques Casanova de Seingalt

[ZHINGOORA BOOKS]

FLIGHT FROM LONDON TO BERLIN

CHAPTER XIV

Bottarelli—A Letter from Pauline—The Avenging Parrot—Pocchini—Guerra, the Venetian—I Meet Sara Again; My Idea of Marrying Her and Settling in Switzerland—The Hanoverians

Thus ended the first act of the comedy; the second began the next morning. I was just getting up, when I heard a noise at the street door, and on putting my head out of the window I saw Pocchini, the scoundrel who had robbed me at Stuttgart trying to get into my house. I cried out wrathfully that I would have nothing to do with him, and slammed down my window.

A little later Goudar put in an appearance. He had got a copy of the St. James's Chronicle, containing a brief report of my arrest, and of my being set a liberty under a bail of eighty guineas. My name and the lady's were disguised, but Rostaing and Bottarelli were set down plainly, and the editor praised their conduct. I felt as if I should like to know Bottarelli, and begged Goudar to take me to him, and Martinelli, happening to call just then, said he would come with us.

We entered a wretched room on the third floor of a wretched house, and there we beheld a picture of the greatest misery. A woman and five children clothed in rags formed the foreground, and in the background was Bottarelli, in an old dressing-gown, writing at a table worthy of Philemon and Baucis. He rose as we came in, and the sight of him moved me to compassion. I said,—

"Do you know me, sir?"

"No, sir, I do not."

"I am Casanova, against whom you bore false witness; whom you tried to cast into Newgate."

"I am very sorry, but look around you and say what choice have I? I have no bread to give my children. I will do as much in your favour another time for nothing."

"Are you not afraid of the gallows?"

"No, for perjury is not punished with death; besides it is very difficult to prove."

"I have heard you are a poet."

"Yes. I have lengthened the Didone and abridged the Demetrio."

"You are a great poet, indeed!"

I felt more contempt than hatred for the rascal, and gave his wife a guinea, for which she presented me with a wretched pamphlet by her husband: "The Secrets of the Freemasons Displayed." Bottarelli had been a monk in his native city, Pisa, and had fled to England with his wife, who had been a nun.

About this time M. de Saa surprised me by giving me a letter from my fair Portuguese, which confirmed the sad fate of poor Clairmont. Pauline said she was married to Count Al——. I was astonished to hear M. de Saa observe that he had known all about Pauline from the moment she arrived in London. That is the hobby of all diplomatists; they like people to believe that they are omniscient. However, M. de Saa was a man of worth and talent, and one could excuse this weakness as an incident inseparable from his profession; while most diplomatists only make themselves ridiculous by their assumption of universal knowledge.

M. de Saa had been almost as badly treated by the Charpillon as myself, and we might have condoled with one another, but the subject was not mentioned.

A few days afterwards, as I was walking idly about, I passed a place called the Parrot Market. As I was amusing myself by looking at these curious birds, I saw a fine young one in a cage, and asked what language it spoke. They told me that it was quite young and did not speak at all yet, so I bought it for ten guineas. I thought I would teach the bird a pretty speech, so I had the cage hung by my bed, and repeated dozens of times every day the following sentence: "The Charpillon is a bigger wh—e than her mother."

The only end I had in view was my private amusement, and in a fortnight the bird had learnt the phrase with the utmost exactness; and every time it uttered the words it accompanied them with a shriek of laughter which I had not taught it, but which made me laugh myself.

One day Gondar heard the bird, and told me that if I sent it to the Exchange I should certainly get fifty guineas for it. I welcomed the idea, and resolved to make the parrot the instrument of my vengeance against the woman who had treated me so badly. I secured myself from fear of the law, which is severe in such cases, by entrusting the bird to my negro, to whom such merchandise was very suitable.

For the first two or three days my parrot did not attract much attention, its observations being in French; but as soon as those who knew the subject of them had heard it, its audience increased and bids were made. Fifty guineas seemed rather too much, and my negro wanted me to lower the price, but I would not agree, having fallen in love with this odd revenge.

In the course of a week Goudar came to inform me of the effect the parrot's criticism had produced in the Charpillon family. As the vendor was my negro, there could be no doubt as to whom it belonged, and who had been its master of languages. Goudar said that the Charpillon thought my vengeance very ingenious, but that the mother and aunts were furious. They had consulted several counsel, who agreed in saying that a parrot could not be indicted for libel, but that they could make me pay dearly for my jest if they could prove that I had been the bird's instructor. Goudar warned me to be careful of owning to the fact, as two witnesses would suffice to undo me.

The facility with which false witnesses may be produced in London is something dreadful. I have myself seen the word evidence written in large characters in a window; this is as much as to say that false witnesses may be procured within.

The St. James's Chronicle contained an article on my parrot, in which the writer remarked that the ladies whom the bird insulted must be very poor and friendless, or they would have bought it at once, and have thus prevented the thing from becoming the talk of the town. He added,—

"The teacher of the parrot has no doubt made the bird an instrument of his vengeance, and has displayed his wit in doing so; he ought to be an Englishman."

I met my good friend Edgar, and asked him why he had not bought the little slanderer.

"Because it delights all who know anything about the object of the slander," said he.

At last Jarbe found a purchaser for fifty guineas, and I heard afterwards that Lord Grosvenor had bought it to please the Charpillon, with whom he occasionally diverted himself.

Thus my relations with that girl came to an end. I have seen her since with the greatest indifference, and without any renewal of the old pain.

One day, as I was going into St. James's Park, I saw two girls drinking milk in a room on the ground floor of a house. They called out to me, but not knowing them I passed on my way. However, a young officer of my acquaintance came after me and said they were Italians, and being curious to see them I retracted my steps.

When I entered the room I was accosted by the scoundrelly Pocchini, dressed in a military uniform, who said he had the honour of introducing me to his daughters.

"Indeed," said I, "I remember two other daughters of yours robbing me of a snuff-box and two watches at Stuttgart."

"You lie!" said the impudent rascal.

I gave him no verbal answer, but took up a glass of milk and flung it in his face, and then left the room without more ado.

I was without my sword. The young officer who had brought me into the place followed me and told me I must not go without giving his friend some satisfaction.

"Tell him to come out, and do you escort him to the Green Park, and I shall have the pleasure of giving him a caning in your presence, unless you would like to fight for him; if so, you must let me go home and get my sword. But do you know this man whom you call your friend?"

"No, but he is an officer, and it is I that brought him here."

"Very good, I will fight to the last drop of my blood; but I warn you your friend is a thief. But go; I will await you."

In the course of a quarter of an hour they all came out, but the Englishman and Pocchini followed me alone. There were a good many people about, and I went before them till we reached Hyde Park. Pocchini attempted to speak to me, but I replied, lifting my cane,—

"Scoundrel, draw your sword, unless you want me to give you a thrashing!"

"I will never draw upon a defenceless man."

I gave him a blow with my cane by way of answer, and the coward, instead of drawing his sword, began to cry out that I wished to draw him into a fight. The Englishman burst out laughing and begged me to pardon his interference, and then, taking me by the arm, said,—

"Come along, sir, I see you know the gentleman."

The coward went off in another direction, grumbling as he went.

On the way I informed the officer of the very good reasons I had for treating Pocchini as a rogue, and he agreed that I had been perfectly right. "Unfortunately," he added, "I am in love with one of his daughters."

When we were in the midst of St. James's Park we saw them, and I could not help laughing when I noticed Goudar with one of them on each side.

"How did you come to know these ladies?" said I.

"Their father the captain," he answered, "has sold me jewels; he introduced me to them."

"Where did you leave our father?" asked one.

"In Hyde Park, after giving him a caning."

"You served him quite right."

The young Englishman was indignant to hear them approving my ill-treatment of their father, and shook my hand and went away, swearing to me that he would never be seen in their company again.

A whim of Goudar's, to which I was weak enough to consent, made me dine with these miserable women in a tavern on the borders of London. The rascally Goudar made them drunk, and in this state they told some terrible truths about their pretended father. He did not live with them, but paid them nocturnal visits in which he robbed them of all the money they had earned. He was their pander, and made them rob their visitors instructing them to pass it off as a joke if the theft was discovered. They gave him the stolen articles, but he never said what he did with them. I could not help laughing at this involuntary confession, remembering what Goudar had said about Pocchini selling him jewels.

After this wretched meal I went away leaving the duty of escorting them back to Goudar. He came and saw me the next day, and informed me that the girls had been arrested and taken to prison just as they were entering their house.

"I have just been to Pocchini's," said he, "but the landlord tells me he has not been in since yesterday."

The worthy and conscientious Goudar added that he did not care if he never saw him again, as he owed the fellow ten guineas for a watch, which his daughters had probably stolen, and which was well worth double.

Four days later I saw him again, and he informed me that the rascal had left London with a servant-maid, whom he had engaged at a registry office where any number of servants are always ready to take service with the first comer. The keeper of the office answers for their fidelity.

"The girl he has gone with is a pretty one, from what the man tells me, and they have taken ship from London. I am sorry he went away before I could pay him for the watch; I am dreading every moment to meet the individual from whom it was stolen."

I never heard what became of the girls, but Pocchini will re-appear on the scene in due course.

I led a tranquil and orderly life, which I should have been pleased to continue for the remainder of my days; but circumstances and my destiny ordered it otherwise, and against these it is not becoming in a Christian philosopher to complain. I went several times to see my daughter at her school, and I also frequented the British Museum, where I met Dr. Mati. One day I found an Anglican minister with him, and I asked the clergyman how many different sects there were in England.

"Sir," he replied in very tolerable Italian, "no one can give a positive answer to that question, for every week some sect dies and some new one is brought into being. All that is necessary is for a man of good faith, or some rogue desirous of money or notoriety, to stand in some frequented place and begin preaching. He explains some texts of the Bible in his own fashion, and if he pleases the gapers around him they invite him to expound next Sunday, often in a tavern. He keeps the appointment and explains his new doctrines in a spirited manner. Then people begin to talk of him; he disputes with ministers of other sects; he and his followers give themselves a name, and the thing is done. Thus, or almost thus, are all the numerous English sects produced."

About this time M. Steffano Guerra, a noble Venetian who was travelling with the leave of his Government, lost a case against an English painter who had executed a miniature painting of one of the prettiest ladies in London, Guerra having given a written promise to pay twenty-five guineas. When it was finished Guerra did not like it, and would not take it or pay the price. The Englishman, in accordance with the English custom, began by arresting his debtor; but Guerra was released on bail, and brought the matter before the courts, which condemned him to pay the twenty-five guineas. He appealed, lost again, and was in the end obliged to pay. Guerra contented that he had ordered a portrait, that a picture bearing no likeness to the lady in question was not a portrait, and that he had therefore a right to refuse payment. The painter replied that it was a portrait as it had been painted from life. The judgment was that the painter must live by his trade, and that as Guerra had given him painting to do he must therefore provide him with the wherewithal to live, seeing that the artist swore he had done his best to catch the likeness. Everybody thought this sentence just, and so did I; but I confess it also seemed rather hard, especially to Guerra, who with costs had to pay a hundred guineas for the miniature.

Malingan's daughter died just as her father received a public box on the ear from a nobleman who liked piquet, but did not like players who corrected the caprices of fortune. I gave the poor wretch the wherewithal to bury his daughter and to leave England. He died soon after at Liège, and his wife told me of the circumstance, saying that he had expired regretting his inability to pay his debts.

M. M—— F—— came to London as the representative of the canton of Berne, and I called, but was not received. I suspected that he had got wind of the liberties I had taken with pretty Sara, and did not want me to have an opportunity for renewing them. He was a somewhat eccentric man, so I did not take offence, and had almost forgotten all about it when chance led me to the Marylebone Theatre one evening. The spectators sat at little tables, and the charge for admittance was only a shilling, but everyone was expected to order something, were it only a pot of ale.

On going into the theatre I chanced to sit down beside a girl whom I did not notice at first, but soon after I came in she turned towards me, and I beheld a ravishing profile which somehow seemed familiar; but I attributed that to the idea of perfect beauty that was graven on my soul. The more I looked at her the surer I felt that I had never seen her before, though a smile of inexpressible slyness had begun to play about her lips. One of her gloves fell, and I hastened to restore it to her, whereupon she thanked me in a few well-chosen French sentences.

"Madam is not English, then?" said I, respectfully.

"No, sir, I am a Swiss, and a friend of yours."

At this I looked round, and on my right hand sat Madame M——— F———, then her eldest daughter, then her husband. I got up, and after bowing to the lady, for whom I had a great esteem, I saluted her husband, who only replied by a slight movement of the head. I asked Madame M——— F——— what her husband had against me, and she said that Possano had written to him telling some dreadful stories about me.

There was not time for me to explain and justify myself, so I devoted all my energies to the task of winning the daughter's good graces. In three years she had grown into a perfect beauty: she knew it, and by her blushes as she spoke to me I knew she was thinking of what had passed between us in the presence of my housekeeper. I was anxious to find out whether she would acknowledge the fact, or deny it altogether. If she had done so I should have despised her. When I had seen her before, the blossom of her beauty was still in the bud, now it had opened out in all its splendour.

"Charming Sara," I said, "you have so enchanted me that I cannot help asking you a couple of questions, which if you value my peace of mind you will answer. Do you remember what happened at Berne?"

"Yes."

"And do you repent of what you did?"

"No."

No man of any delicacy could ask the third question, which may be understood. I felt sure that Sara would make me happy—nay, that she was even longing for the moment, and gave reins to my passions, determined to convince her that I was deserving of her love. The waiter came to enquire if we had any orders, and I begged Madame M—— F—— to allow me to offer her some oysters. After the usual polite refusals she gave in, and I profited by her acceptance to order all the delicacies of the season, including a hare (a great delicacy in London), champagne, choice liqueurs, larks, ortolans, truffles, sweetmeats—everything, in fact, that money could buy, and I was not at all surprised when the bill proved to amount to ten guineas. But I was very much surprised when M. M—— F——, who had eaten like a Turk and drunk like a Swiss, said calmly that it was too dear.

I begged him politely not to trouble himself about the cost; and by way of proving that I did not share his opinion, I gave the waiter half-a-guinea; the worthy man looked as if he wished that such customers came more often. The Swiss, who had been pale and gloomy enough a short while before, was rubicund and affable. Sara glanced at me and squeezed my hand; I had conquered.

When the play was over, M—— F—— asked me if I would allow him to call on me. I embraced him in reply. His servant came in, and said that he could not find a coach; and I, feeling rather surprised that he had not brought his carriage, offered him the use of mine, telling my man to get me a sedan-chair.

"I accept your kind offer," said he, "on the condition that you allow me to occupy the chair."

I consented to this arrangement, and took the mother and the two daughters with me in the carriage.

On the way, Madame M—— F—— was very polite, gently blaming her husband for the rudeness of which I had to complain. I said that I would avenge myself by paying an assiduous court to him in the future; but she pierced me to the heart by saying that they were on the point of departing. "We wanted to go on the day after next," she said, "and to-morrow we shall have to leave our present rooms to their new occupants. A matter of business which my husband was not able to conclude will oblige us to stay for another week, and to-morrow we shall have the double task of moving and finding new apartments."

"Then you have not yet got new rooms?"

"No, but my husband says he is certain to find some to-morrow morning."

"Furnished, I suppose, for as you intend to leave you will be selling, your furniture."

"Yes, and we shall have to pay the expenses of carriage to the buyer."

On hearing that M. M—— F—— was sure of finding lodgings, I was precluded from offering to accommodate them in my own house, as the lady might think that I only made the offer because I was sure it would not be accepted.

When we got to the door of their house we alighted, and the mother begged me to come in. She and her husband slept on the second floor, and the two girls on the third. Everything was upside down, and as Madame M—— F—— had something to say to the landlady she asked me to go up with her daughters. It was cold, and the room we entered had no fire in it. The sister went into the room adjoining and I stayed with Sara, and all of a sudden I clasped her to my breast, and feeling that her desires were as ardent as mine I fell with her on to a sofa where we mingled our beings in all the delights of voluptuous ardours. But this happiness was short lived; scarcely was the work achieved when we heard a footstep on the stair. It was the father.

If M—— F—— had had any eyes he must have found us out, for my face bore the marks of agitation, the nature of which it was easy to divine. We exchanged a few brief compliments; I shook his hand and disappeared. I was in such a state of excitement when I got home that I made up my mind to leave England and to follow Sara to Switzerland. In the night I formed my plans, and resolved to offer the family my house during the time they stayed in England, and if necessary to force them to accept my offer.

In the morning I hastened to call on M—— F——, and found him on his doorstep.

"I am going to try and get a couple of rooms," said he.

"They are already found," I replied. "My house is at your service, and you must give me the preference. Let us come upstairs."

"Everybody is in bed."

"Never mind," said I, and we proceeded to go upstairs.

Madame M—— F—— apologized for being in bed. Her husband told her that I wanted to let them some rooms, but I laughed and said I desired they would accept my hospitality as that of a friend. After some polite denials my offer was accepted, and it was agreed that the whole family should take up their quarters with me in the evening.

I went home, and was giving the necessary orders when I was told that two young ladies wished to see me. I went down in person, and I was agreeably surprised to see Sara and her sister. I asked them to come in, and Sara told me that the landlady would not let their belongings out of the house before her father paid a debt of forty guineas, although a city merchant had assured her it should be settled in a week. The long and snort of it was that Sara's father had sent me a bill and begged me to discount it.

I took the bill and gave her a bank note for fifty pounds in exchange, telling her that she could give me the change another time. She thanked me with great simplicity and went her way, leaving me delighted with the confidence she had placed in me.

The fact of M. M—— F——'s wanting forty guineas did not make me divine that he was in some straits, for I looked at everything through rose-coloured glasses, and was only too happy to be of service to him.

I made a slight dinner in order to have a better appetite for supper, and spent the afternoon in writing letters. In the evening M. M—— F——'s man came with three great trunks and innumerable card-board boxes, telling me that the family would soon follow;

but I awaited them in vain till nine o'clock. I began to get alarmed and went to the house, where I found them all in a state of consternation. Two ill-looking fellows who were in the room enlightened me; and assuming a jovial and unconcerned air, I said,—

"I'll wager, now, that this is the work of some fierce creditor."

"You are right," answered the father, "but I am sure of discharging the debt in five or six days, and that's why I put off my departure."

"Then you were arrested after you had sent on your trunks."

"Just after."

"And what have you done?"

"I have sent for bail."

"Why did you not send to me?"

"Thank you, I am grateful for your kindness, but you are a foreigner, and sureties have to be householders."

"But you ought to have told me what had happened, for I have got you an excellent supper, and I am dying of hunger."

It was possible that this debt might exceed my means, so I did not dare to offer to pay it. I took Sara aside, and on hearing that all his trouble was on account of a debt of a hundred and fifty pounds, I asked the bailiff whether we could go away if the debt was paid.

"Certainly," said he, shewing me the bill of exchange.

I took out three bank notes of fifty pounds each, and gave them to the man, and taking the bill I said to the poor Swiss,—

"You shall pay me the money before you leave England."

The whole family wept with joy, and after embracing them all I summoned them to come and sup with me and forget the troubles of life.

We drove off to my house and had a merry supper, though the worthy mother could not quite forget her sadness. After supper I took them to the rooms which had been prepared for them, and with which they were delighted, and so I wished them good night, telling them that they should be well entertained till their departure, and that I hoped to follow them into Switzerland.

When I awoke the next day I was in a happy frame of mind. On examining my desires I found that they had grown too strong to be overcome, but I did not wish to overcome them. I loved Sara, and I felt so certain of possessing her that I put all desires out of my mind; desires are born only of doubt, and doubt torments the soul. Sara was mine; she had given herself to me out of pure passion, without any shadow of self-interest.

I went to the father's room, and found him engaged in opening his trunks. His wife looked sad, so I asked her if she were not well. She replied that her health was perfect, but that the thought of the sea voyage troubled her sorely. The father begged me to excuse him at breakfast as he had business to attend to. The two young ladies came down, and after we had breakfast I asked the mother why they were unpacking their trunks so short a time before starting. She smiled and said that one trunk would be ample for all their possessions, as they had resolved to sell all superfluities. As I had seen some beautiful dresses, fine linen, and exquisite lace, I could not refrain from saying that it would be a great pity to sell cheaply what would have to be replaced dearly.

"You are right," she said, "but, nevertheless, there is no pleasure so great as the consciousness of having paid one's debts."

"You must not sell anything," I replied, in a lively manner, "for as I am going to Switzerland with you I can pay your debts, and you shall repay me when you can."

At these words astonishment was depicted on her face.

"I did not think you were speaking seriously," said she.

"Perfectly seriously, and here is the object of my vows."

With these words I seized Sara's hand and covered it with kisses.

Sara blushed, said nothing, and the mother looked kindly at us; but after a moment's silence she spoke at some length, and with the utmost candour and wisdom. She gave me circumstantial information as to the position of the family and her husband's restricted means, saying that under the circumstances he could not have avoided running into debt, but that he had done wrong to bring them all with him to London.

"If he had been by himself," she said, "he could have lived here comfortably enough with only one servant, but with a family to provide for the two thousand crowns per annum provided by the Government are quite insufficient. My old father has succeeded in persuading the State to discharge my husband's debts, but to make up the extra expense they will not employ a Charge d'affaires; a banker with the title of agent will collect the interest on their English securities."

She ended by saying that she thought Sara was fortunate to have pleased me, but that she was not sure whether her husband would consent to the marriage.

The word "marriage" made Sara blush, and I was pleased, though it was evident there would be difficulties in the way.

M—— F—— came back and told his wife that two clothes dealers would come to purchase their superfluous clothes in the afternoon; but after explaining my ideas I had not much trouble in convincing him that it would be better not to sell them, and that he could become my debtor to the amount of two hundred pounds, on which he could pay interest till he was able to return me my capital. The agreement was written out the same day, but I did not mention the marriage question, as his wife had told me she would discuss it with him in private.

On the third day he came down by himself to talk with me.

"My wife," he began, "has told me of your intentions, and I take it as a great honour, I assure you; but I cannot give you my Sara, as she is promised to M. de W——, and family reasons prevent me from going back from my word. Besides my old father, a strict Calvinist, would object to the difference in religion. He would never believe that his dear little grandchild would be happy with a Roman Catholic."

As a matter of fact I was not at all displeased at what he said. I was certainly very fond of Sara, but the word "marriage" had a disagreeable sound to me. I answered that circumstances might change in time, and that in the meanwhile I should be quite content if he would allow me to be the friend of the family and to take upon myself all the responsibility of the journey. He promised everything, and assured me that he was delighted at his daughter having won my affection.

After this explanation I gave Sara as warm marks of my love as decency would allow in the presence of her father and mother, and I could see that all the girl thought of was love.

The fifth day I went up to her room, and finding her in bed all the fires of passion flamed up in my breast, for since my first visit to their house I had not been alone with her. I threw myself upon her, covering her with kisses, and she shewed herself affectionate but reserved. In vain I endeavoured to succeed; she opposed a gentle resistance to my efforts, and though she caressed me, she would not let me attain my end.

"Why, divine Sara," said I, "do you oppose my loving ecstasy?"

"Dearest, I entreat of you not to ask for any more than I am willing to give."

"Then you no longer love me?"

"Cruel man, I adore you!"

"Then why do you treat me to a refusal, after having once surrendered unreservedly?"

"I have given myself to you, and we have both been happy, and I think that should be enough for us."

"There must be some reason for this change. If you love me, dearest Sara, this renunciation must be hard for you to bear."

"I confess it, but nevertheless I feel it is my duty. I have made up my mind to subdue my passion from no weak motive, but from a sense of what I owe to myself. I am under obligations to you, and if I were to repay the debt I have contracted with my body I should be degraded in my own eyes. When we enjoyed each other before only love was between us—there was no question of debit and credit. My heart is now the thrall of what I owe you, and to these debts it will not give what it gave so readily to love."

"This is a strange philosophy, Sara; believe me it is fallacious, and the enemy of your happiness as well as mine. These sophisms lead you astray and wound me to the heart. Give me some credit for delicacy of feeling, and believe me you owe me nothing."

"You must confess that if you had not loved me you would have done nothing for my father."

"Certainly I will confess nothing of the kind; I would readily do as much, and maybe more, out of regard for your worthy mother. It is quite possible, indeed, that in doing this small service for your father I had no thoughts of you at all."

"It might be so; but I do not believe it was so. Forgive me, dearest, but I cannot make up my mind to pay my debts in the way you wish."

"It seems to me that if you are grateful to me your love ought to be still more ardent."

"It cannot be more ardent than it is already."

"Do you know how grievously you make me suffer?"

"Alas! I suffer too; but do not reproach me; let us love each other still."

This dialogue is not the hundredth part of what actually passed between us till dinner-time. The mother came in, and finding me seated at the foot of the daughter's bed, laughed, and asked me why I kept her in bed. I answered with perfect coolness that we had been so interested in our conversation that we had not noticed the flight of time.

I went to dress, and as I thought over the extraordinary change which had taken place in Sara I resolved that it should not last for long. We dined together gaily, and Sara and I behaved in all respects like two lovers. In the evening I took them to the Italian Opera, coming home to an excellent supper.

The next morning I passed in the city, having accounts to settle with my bankers. I got some letters of exchange on Geneva, and said farewell to the worthy Mr. Bosanquet. In the afternoon I got a coach for Madame M—— F—— to pay some farewells calls, and I went to say good-bye to my daughter at school. The dear little girl burst into tears, saying that she would be lost without me, and begging me not to forget her. I was deeply moved. Sophie begged me to go and see her mother before I left England, and I decided on doing so.

At supper we talked over our journey, and M. M—— F—— agreed with me that it would be better to go by Dunkirk than Ostend. He had very little more business to attend to. His debts were paid, and he said he thought he would have a matter of fifty guineas in his pocket at the journey's end, after paying a third share of all the travelling expenses. I had to agree to this, though I made up my mind at the same time not to let him see any of the accounts. I hoped to win Sara, in one way or another, when we got to Berne.

The next day, after breakfast, I took her hand in presence of her mother, and asked her if she would give me her heart if I could obtain her father's consent at Berne.

"Your mother," I added, "has promised me that hers shall not be wanting."

At this the mother got up, and saying that we had no doubt a good deal to talk over, she and her eldest daughter went out to pay some calls.

As soon as we were alone Sara said that she could not understand how I could have the smallest doubt as to whether her consent would be given.

"I have shewn you how well I love you," said she, tenderly; "and I am sure I should be very happy as your wife. You may be sure that your wishes will be mine, and that, however far you lead me, Switzerland shall claim no thought of mine."

I pressed the amorous Sara to my bosom in a transport of delight, which was shared by her; but as she saw me grow more ardent she begged me to be moderate. Clasping me in her arms she adjured me not to ask her for that which she was determined not to grant till she was mine by lawful wedlock.

"You will drive me to despair! Have you reflected that this resistance may cost me my life? Can you love, and yet entertain this fatal prejudice? And yet I am sure you love me, and pleasure too."

"Yes, dearest one, I do love you, and amorous pleasure with you; but you must respect my delicacy."

My eyes were wet with tears, and she was so affected that she fell fainting to the ground. I lifted her up and gently laid her on the bed. Her pallor alarmed me. I brought smelling-salts, I rubbed her forehead with Savoy-water, and she soon opened her eyes, and seemed delighted to find me calm again.

The thought of taking advantage of her helplessness would have horrified me. She sat up on the bed, and said,—

"You have just given a true proof of the sincerity of your affection."

"Did you think, sweetheart, that I was vile enough to abuse your weakness? Could I enjoy a pleasure in which you had no share?"

"I did not think you would do such a thing, but I should not have resisted, though it is possible that I should not have loved you afterwards."

"Sara, though you do not know, you charm my soul out of my body."

After this I sat down sadly on the bed, and abandoned myself to the most melancholy reflections, from which Sara did not endeavour to rouse me.

Her mother came in and asked why she was on the bed, but not at all suspiciously. Sara told her the truth.

M. M—— F—— came in soon after, and we dined together, but silently. What I had heard from the girl's lips had completely overwhelmed me. I saw I had nothing to hope for, and that it was time for me to look to myself. Six weeks before, God had delivered me from my bondage to an infamous woman, and now I was in danger of becoming the slave of an angel. Such were my reflections whilst Sara was fainting, but it was necessary for me to consider the matter at my leisure.

There was a sale of valuable articles in the city, the means taken for disposing of them being a lottery. Sara had read the announcement, and I asked her with her mother and sister to come with me and take part in it. I had not much trouble in obtaining their consent, and we found ourselves in distinguished company, among the persons present being the Countess of Harrington, Lady Stanhope, and Emilie and her daughters. Emilie had a strange case before the courts. She had given information to the police that her husband had been robbed of six thousand pounds, though everyone said that she herself was the thief.

Madame M—— F—— did not take a ticket, but she allowed me to take tickets for her daughters, who were in high glee, since for ten or twelve guineas they got articles worth sixty.

Every day I was more taken with Sara; but feeling sure that I should only obtain slight favours from her, I thought it was time to come to an explanation. So after supper I said that as it was not certain that Sara could become my wife I had determined not to accompany them to Berne. The father told me I was very wise, and that I could still correspond with his daughter, Sara said nothing, but I could see she was much grieved.

I passed a dreadful night; such an experience was altogether new to me. I weighed Sara's reasons, and they seemed to me to be merely frivolous, which drove me to conclude that my caresses had displeased her.

For the last three days I found myself more than once alone with her; but I was studiously moderate, and she caressed me in a manner that would have made my bliss if I had not already obtained the one great favour. It was at this time I learnt the truth of the maxim that if abstinence is sometimes the spur of love, it has also the contrary effect. Sara had brought my feeling to a pitch of gentle friendship, while an infamous prostitute like the

Charpillon, who knew how to renew hope and yet grant nothing, ended by inspiring me with contempt, and finally with hatred.

The family sailed for Ostend, and I accompanied them to the mouth of the Thames. I gave Sara a letter for Madame de W——. This was the name of the learned Hedvig whom she did not know. They afterwards became sisters-in-law, as Sara married a brother of M. de W——, and was happy with him.

Even now I am glad to hear tidings of my old friends and their doings, but the interest I take in such matters is not to be compared to my interest in some obscure story of ancient history. For our contemporaries, the companions, of our youthful follies, we have a kind of contempt, somewhat similar to that which we entertain for ourselves. Four years ago I wrote to Madame G—— at Hamburg, and my letter began:

"After a silence of twenty-one years . . ."

She did not deign to reply, and I was by no means displeased. We cared no longer for one another, and it is quite natural that it should be so.

When I tell my reader who Madame G—— is, he will be amused. Two years ago I set out for Hamburg, but my good genius made me turn back to Dux; what had I to do at Hamburg?

After my guests were gone I went to the Italian Opera at Covent Garden, and met Goudar, who asked me if I would come to the Sartori's concert. He told me I should see a beautiful young English woman there who spoke Italian. As I had just lost Sara I did not much care about making new acquaintances, but still I was curious to see the young marvel. I indulged my curiosity, and I am glad to say that instead of being amused I was wearied, though the young English woman was pretty enough. A young Livonian, who called himself Baron of Stenau, seemed extremely interested in her. After supper she offered us tickets for the next concert, and I took one for myself and one for Gondar, giving her two guineas, but the Livonian baron took fifty tickets, and gave her a bank note for fifty guineas. I saw by this that he wanted to take the place by storm, and I liked his way of doing it. I supposed him to be rich, without caring to enquire into his means. He made advances to me and we became friends, and the reader will see in due time what a fatal acquaintance he was.

One day as I was walking with Goudar in Hyde Park he left me to speak to two ladies who seemed pretty.

He was not long absent, and said, when he rejoined me,—

"A Hanoverian lady, a widow and the mother of five daughters, came to England two months ago with her whole family. She lives close by, and is occupied in soliciting compensation from the Government for any injury that was done her by the passage of the Duke of Cumberland's army. The mother herself is sick and and never leaves her bed; she sends her two eldest daughters to petition the Government, and they are the two young ladies you have just seen. They have not met with any success. The eldest daughter is twenty-two, and the youngest fourteen; they are all pretty and can speak English, French, and German equally well, and are always glad to see visitors. I had been to visit them myself, but as I gave them nothing I do not care to go there alone a second time. If you like, however, I can introduce you."

"You irritate my curiosity. Come along, but if the one that pleases me is not complaisant she shall have nothing."

"They will not even allow one to take them by the hand."

"They are Charpillons, I suppose."

"It looks like it. But you won't see any men there:"

We were shewn into a large room where I noticed three pretty girls and an evil-looking man. I began with the usual compliments, to which the girls replied politely, but with an air of great sadness.

Goudar spoke to the man, and then came to me shrugging his shoulders, and saying,—

"We have come at a sad time. That man is a bailiff who has come to take the mother to prison if she can't pay her landlord the twenty guineas' rent she owes him, and they haven't got a farthing. When the mother has been sent to prison the landlord will no doubt turn the girls out of doors."

"They can live with their mother for nothing."

"Not at all. If they have got the money they can have their meals in prison, but no one is allowed to live in a prison except the prisoners."

I asked one of them where her sisters were.

"They have gone out, to look for money, for the landlord won't accept any surety, and we have nothing to sell."

"All this is very sad; what does your mother say?"

"She only weeps, and yet, though she is ill and cannot leave her bed, they are going to take her to prison. By way of consolation the landlord says he will have her carried."

"It is very hard. But your looks please me, mademoiselle, and if you will be kind I may be able to extricate you from the difficulty."

"I do not know what you mean by 'kind.'"

"Your mother will understand; go and ask her."

"Sir, you do not know us; we are honest girls, and ladies of position besides."

With these words the young woman turned her back on me, and began to weep again. The two others, who were quite as pretty, stood straight up and said not a word. Goudar whispered to me in Italian that unless we did something for them we should cut but a sorry figure there; and I was cruel enough to go away without saying a word.

CHAPTER XV

The Hanoverians

As we were leaving the house we met the two eldest sisters, who came home looking very sad. I was struck by their beauty, and extremely surprised to hear myself greeted by one of them, who said,—

"It is M. the Chevalier de Seingalt."

"Himself, mademoiselle, and sorely grieved at your misfortune."

"Be kind enough to come in again for a moment."

"I am sorry to say that I have an important engagement."

"I will not keep you for longer than a quarter of an hour."

I could not refuse so small a favour, and she employed the time in telling me how unfortunate they had been in Hanover, how they had come to London to obtain compensation, of their failure, their debts, the cruelty of the landlord, their mother's illness, the prison that awaited her, the likelihood of their being cast into the street, and the cruelty of all their acquaintances.

"We have nothing to sell, and all our resources consist of two shillings, which we shall have to spend on bread, on which we live."

"Who are your friends? How can they abandon you at such a time?"

She mentioned several names—among others, Lord Baltimore, Marquis

Carracioli, the Neapolitan ambassador, and Lord Pembroke.

"I can't believe it," said I, "for I know the two last noblemen to be both rich and generous. There must be some good reason for their conduct, since you are beautiful; and for these gentlemen beauty is a bill to be honoured on sight."

"Yes, there is a reason. These rich noblemen abandon us with contempt. They refuse to take pity on us because we refuse to yield to their guilty passion."

"That is to say, they have taken a fancy to you, and as you will not have pity on them they refuse to have pity on you. Is it not so?"

"That is exactly the situation."

"Then I think they are in the right."

"In the right?"

"Yes, I am quite of their opinion. We leave you to enjoy your sense of virtue, and we spend our money in procuring those favours which you refuse us. Your misfortune really is your prettiness, if you were ugly you would get twenty guineas fast enough. I would give you the money myself, and the action would be put down to benevolence; whereas, as the case stands, if I were to give you anything it would be thought that I was actuated by the hope of favours to come, and I should be laughed at, and deservedly, as a dupe."

I felt that this was the proper way to speak to the girl, whose eloquence in pleading her cause was simply wonderful.

She did not reply to my oration, and I asked her how she came to know me.

"I saw you at Richmond with the Charpillon."

"She cost me two thousand guineas, and I got nothing for my money; but I have profited by the lesson, and in future I shall never pay in advance."

Just then her mother called her, and, begging me to wait a moment, she went into her room, and returned almost directly with the request that I would come and speak to the invalid.

I found her sitting up in her bed; she looked about forty-five, and still preserved traces of her former beauty; her countenance bore the imprint of sadness, but had no marks of sickness whatsoever. Her brilliant and expressive eyes, her intellectual face, and a suggestion of craft about her, all bade me be on my guard, and a sort of false likeness to the Charpillon's mother made me still more cautious, and fortified me in my resolution to give no heed to the appeals of pity.

"Madam," I began, "what can I do for you?"

"Sir," she replied, "I have heard the whole of your conversations with my daughters, and you must confess that you have not talked to them in a very fatherly manner."

"Quite so, but the only part which I desire to play with them is that of lover, and a fatherly style would not have been suitable to the part. If I had the happiness of being their father, the case would be altered. What I have said to your daughters is what I feel, and what I think most likely to bring about the end I have in view. I have not the slightest pretence to virtue, but I adore the fair sex, and now you and they know the road to my purse. If they wish to preserve their virtue, why let them; nobody will trouble them, and they, on their side, must not expect anything from men. Good-bye, madam; you may reckon on my never addressing your daughters again."

"Wait a moment, sir. My husband was the Count of——, and you see that my daughters are of respectable birth."

"Have you not pity for our situation?"

"I pity you extremely, and I would relieve you in an instant if your daughters were ugly, but as it is they are pretty, and that alters the case."

"What an argument!"

"It is a very strong one with me, and I think I am the best judge of arguments which apply to myself. You want twenty guineas; well, you shall have them after one of your five countesses has spent a joyous night with me."

"What language to a woman of my station! Nobody has ever dared to speak to me in such a way before."

"Pardon me, but what use is rank without a halfpenny? Allow me to retire.

"To-day we have only bread to eat."

"Well, certainly that is rather hard on countesses."

"You are laughing at the title, apparently."

"Yes, I am; but I don't want to offend you. If you like, I will stop to dinner, and pay for all, yourself included."

"You are an eccentric individual. My girls are sad, for I am going to prison. You will find their company wearisome."

"That is my affair."

"You had much better give them the money you would spend on the dinner."

"No, madam. I must have at least the pleasures of sight and sound for my money. I will stay your arrest till to-morrow, and afterwards Providence may possibly intervene on your behalf."

"The landlord will not wait."

"Leave me to deal with him."

I told Goudar to go and see what the man would take to send the bailiff away for twenty-four hours. He returned with the message that he must have a guinea and bail for the twenty guineas, in case the lodgers might take to flight before the next day.

My wine merchant lived close by. I told Gondar to wait for me, and the matter was soon settled and the bailiff sent away, and I told the five girls that they might take their ease for twenty-four hours more.

I informed Gondar of the steps I had taken, and told him to go out and get a good dinner for eight people. He went on his errand, and I summoned the girls to their mother's bedside, and delighted them all by telling them that for the next twenty-four hours they were to make good cheer. They could not get over their surprise at the suddenness of the change I had worked in the house.

"But this is all I can do for you," said I to the mother. "Your daughters are charming, and I have obtained a day's respite for you all without asking for anything in return; I shall dine, sup, and pass the night with them without asking so much as a single kiss, but if your ideas have not changed by to-morrow you will be in exactly the same position as you were a few minutes ago, and I shall not trouble you any more with my attentions."

"What do you mean my 'changing my ideas'?"

"I need not tell you, for you know perfectly well what I mean."

"My daughters shall never become prostitutes."

"I will proclaim their spotless chastity all over London—but I shall spend my guineas elsewhere."

"You are a cruel man."

"I confess I can be very cruel, but it is only when I don't meet with kindness."

Goudar came back and we returned to the ladies' room, as the mother did not like to shew herself to my friend, telling me that I was the only man she had permitted to see her in bed during the whole time she had been in London.

Our English dinner was excellent in its way, but my chief pleasure was to see the voracity with which the girls devoured the meal. One would have thought they were savages devouring raw meat after a long fast. I had got a case of excellent wine and I made each of them drink a bottle, but not being accustomed to such an indulgence they became quite drunk. The mother had devoured the whole of the plentiful helpings I had sent in to her, and she had emptied a bottle of Burgundy, which she carried very well.

In spite of their intoxication, the girls were perfectly safe; I kept my word, and Goudar did not take the slightest liberty. We had a pleasant supper, and after a bowl of punch I left them feeling in love with the whole bevy, and very uncertain whether I should be able to shew as brave a front the next day.

As we were going away Goudar said that I was conducting the affair admirably, but if I made a single slip I should be undone.

I saw the good sense of his advice, and determined to shew that I was as sharp as he.

The next day, feeling anxious to hear the result of the council which the mother had doubtless held with the daughters, I called at their house at ten o'clock. The two eldest sisters were out, endeavouring to beat up some more friends, and the three youngest rushed up to me as if they had been spaniels and I their master, but they would not even allow me to kiss them. I told them they made a mistake, and knocked at the mother's door. She told me to come in, and thanked me for the happy day I had given them.

"Am I to withdraw my bail, countess?"

"You can do what you like, but I do not think you capable of such an action."

"You are mistaken. You have doubtless made a deep study of the human heart; but you either know little of the human mind, or else you think you have a larger share than any other person. All your daughters have inspired me with love, but were it a matter of life and death I would not do a single thing for them or you before you have done me the only favour that is in your power. I leave you to your reflections, and more especially to your virtues."

She begged me to stay, but I did not even listen to her. I passed by the three charmers, and after telling my wine merchant to withdraw his security I went in a furious mood to call on Lord Pembroke. As soon as I mentioned the Hanoverians he burst out laughing, and said these false innocents must be made to fulfil their occupation in a proper manner.

"They came whining to me yesterday," he proceeded, "and I not only would not give them anything, but I laughed them to scorn. They have got about twelve guineas out of me on false pretences; they are as cunning sluts as the Charpillon."

I told him what I had done the day before, and what I intended to offer: twenty guineas for the first, and as much for each of the others, but nothing to be paid in advance.

"I had the same idea myself, but I cried off, and I don't think you'll succeed, as Lord Baltimore offered them forty apiece; that is two hundred guineas in all, and the bargain has fallen through because they want the money to be paid in advance. They paid him a visit yesterday, but found him pitiless, for he has been taken in several times by them."

"We shall see what will happen when the mother is under lock and key;
I'll bet we shall have them cheaply."

I came home for dinner, and Goudar, who had just been at their house, reported that the bailiff would only wait till four o'clock, that the two eldest daughters had come back empty-handed, and that they had been obliged to sell one of their dresses to buy a morsel of bread.

I felt certain that they would have recourse to me again, and I was right. We were at dessert when they put in an appearance. I made them sit down, and the eldest sister exhausted her eloquence to persuade me to give them another three days' grace.

"You will find me insensible," said I, "unless you are willing to adopt my plan. If you wish to hear it, kindly follow me into the next room."

She did so, leaving her sister with Goudar, and making her sit down on a sofa beside me, I shewed her twenty guineas, saying,—

"These are yours; but you know on what terms?"

She rejected my offer with disdain, and thinking she might wish to salve her virtue by being attacked, I set to work; but finding her resistance serious I let her alone, and begged her to leave my house immediately. She called to her sister, and they both went out.

In the evening, as I was going to the play, I called on my wine merchant to hear the news. He told me that the mother had been taken to prison, and that the youngest daughter had gone with her; but he did not know what had become of the four others.

I went home feeling quite sad, and almost reproaching myself for not having taken compassion on then; however, just as I was sitting down to supper they appeared before me like four Magdalens. The eldest, who was the orator of the company, told me that their mother was in prison, and that they would have to pass the night in the street if I did not take pity on them.

"You shall have rooms, beds, and good fires," said I, "but first let me see you eat."

Delight appeared on every countenance, and I had numerous dishes brought for them. They ate eagerly but sadly, and only drank water.

"Your melancholy and your abstinence displeases me," said I, to the eldest girl; "go upstairs and you will find everything necessary for your comfort, but take care to be gone at seven in the morning and not to let me see your faces again."

They went up to the second floor without a word.

An hour afterwards, just as I was going to bed, the eldest girl came into my room and said she wished to have a private interview with me. I told my negro to withdraw, and asked her to explain herself.

"What will you do for us," said she, "if I consent to share your couch?"

"I will give you twenty guineas, and I will lodge and board you as long as you give me satisfaction."

Without saying a word she began to undress, and got into bed. She was submissive and nothing more, and did not give me so much as a kiss. At the end of a quarter of an hour I was disgusted with her and got up, and giving her a bank note for twenty guineas I told her to put on her clothes and go back to her room.

"You must all leave my house to-morrow," I said, "for I am ill pleased with you. Instead of giving yourself up for love you have prostituted yourself. I blush for you."

She obeyed mutely, and I went to sleep in an ill humour.

At about seven o'clock in the morning I was awakened by a hand shaking me gently. I opened my eyes, and I was surprised to see the second daughter.

"What do you want?" I said, coldly.

"I want you to take pity on us, and shelter us in your house for a few days longer. I will be very grateful. My sister has told me all, you are displeased with her, but you must forgive her, for her heart is not her own. She is in love with an Italian who is in prison for debt."

"And I suppose you are in love with someone else?"

"No, I am not."

"Could you love me?"

She lowered her eyes, and pressed my hand gently. I drew her towards me, and embraced her, and as I felt her kisses answer mine, I said,—

"You have conquered."

"My name is Victoire."

"I like it, and I will prove the omen a true one."

Victoire, who was tender and passionate, made me spend two delicious hours, which compensated me for my bad quarter of an hour of the night before.

When our exploits were over, I said,—

"Dearest Victoire, I am wholly throe. Let your mother be brought here as soon as she is free. Here are twenty guineas for you."

She did not expect anything, and the agreeable surprise made her in an ecstasy; she could not speak, but her heart was full of happiness. I too was happy, and I believed that a great part of my happiness was caused by the knowledge that I had done a good deed. We are queer creatures all of us, whether we are bad or good. From that moment I gave my servants orders to lay the table for eight persons every day, and told them that I was only at home to Goudar. I spent money madly, and felt that I was within a measurable distance of poverty.

At noon the mother came in a sedan-chair, and went to bed directly. I went to see her, and did not evince any surprise when she began to thank me for my noble generosity. She wanted me to suppose that she thought I had given her daughters forty guineas for nothing, and I let her enjoy her hypocrisy.

In the evening I took them to Covent Garden, where the castrato Tenducci surprised me by introducing me to his wife, of whom he had two children. He laughed at people who said that a castrato could not procreate. Nature had made him a monster that he might remain a man; he was born triorchis, and as only two of the seminal glands had been destroyed the remaining one was sufficient to endow him with virility.

When I got back to my small seraglio I supped merrily with the five nymphs, and spent a delicious night with Victoire, who was overjoyed at having made my conquest. She told me that her sister's lover was a Neapolitan, calling himself Marquis de Petina, and that they were to get married as soon as he was out of prison. It seemed he was expecting remittances, and the mother would be delighted to see her daughter a marchioness.

"How much does the marquis owe?"

"Twenty guineas."

"And the Neapolitan ambassador allows him to languish in prison for such a beggarly sum? I can't believe it."

"The ambassador won't have anything to do with him, because he left
Naples without the leave of the Government."

"Tell your sister that if the ambassador assures me that her lover's name is really the Marquis de Petina, I will get him out of prison immediately."

I went out to ask my daughter, and another boarder of whom I was very fond, to dinner, and on my way called on the Marquis of Caraccioli, an agreeable man, whose acquaintance I had made at Turin. I found the famous Chevalier d'Eon at his house, and I had no need of a private interview to make my inquiries about Petina.

"The young man is really what he professes to me," said the ambassador, "but I will neither receive him nor give him any money till I hear from my Government that he has received leave to travel."

That was enough for me, and I stayed there for an hour listening to d'Eon's amusing story.

Eon had deserted the embassy on account of ten thousand francs which the department of foreign affairs at Versailles had refused to allow him, though the money was his by right. He had placed himself under the protection of the English laws, and after securing two thousand subscribers at a guinea apiece, he had sent to press a huge volume in quarto containing all the letters he had received from the French Government for the last five or six years.

About the same time a London banker had deposited the sum of twenty thousand guineas at the Bank of England, being ready to wager that sum that Eon was a woman. The bet was taken by a number of persons who had formed themselves into a kind of company for the purpose, and the only way to decide it was that Eon should be examined in the presence of witnesses. The chevalier was offered half the wager, but he laughed them to scorn. He said that such an examination would dishonour him, were he man or woman. Caraccioli said that it could only dishonour him if he were a woman, but I could not agree with this opinion. At the end of a year the bet was declared off; but in the course of three years he received his pardon from the king, and appeared at Court in woman's dress, wearing the cross of St. Louis.

Louis XV. had always been aware of the chevalier's sex, but Cardinal Fleuri had taught him that it became kings to be impenetrable, and Louis remained so all his life.

When I got home I gave the eldest Hanoverian twenty guineas, telling her to fetch her marquis out of prison, and bring him to dine with us, as I wanted to know him. I thought she would have died with joy.

The third sister, having taken counsel with Victoire, and doubtless with her mother also, determined to earn twenty guineas for herself, and she had not much trouble in doing so. She it was on whom Lord Pembroke had cast the eye of desire.

These five girls were like five dishes placed before a gourmand, who enjoys them one after the other. To my fancy the last was always the best. The third sister's name was Augusta.

Next Sunday I had a large number of guests. There were my daughter and her friend, Madame Cornelis, and her son. Sophie was kissed and caressed by the Hanoverians, while I bestowed a hundred kisses on Miss Nancy Steyne, who was only thirteen, but whose young beauty worked sad havoc with my senses. My affection was supposed to be fatherly in its character, but, alas I it was of a much more fleshly kind. This Miss Nancy, who seemed to me almost divine, was the daughter of a rich merchant. I said that I wanted to make her father's acquaintance, and she replied that her father proposed coming to call on me that very day. I was delighted to hear of the coincidence, and gave order that he should be shewn in as soon as he came.

The poor marquis was the only sad figure in the company. He was young and well-made, but thin and repulsively ugly. He thanked me for my kindness, saying that I had done a wise thing, as he felt sure the time would come when he would repay me a hundredfold.

I had given my daughter six guineas to buy a pelisse, and she took me to my bedroom to shew it me. Her mother followed her to congratulate me on my seraglio.

At dinner gaiety reigned supreme. I sat between my daughter and Miss Nancy Steyne, and felt happy. Mr. Steyne came in as we were at the oysters. He kissed his daughter with that tender affection which is more characteristic, I think, of English parents than those of any other nation.

Mr. Steyne had dined, but he nevertheless ate a hundred scolloped oysters, in the preparation of which my cook was wonderfully expert; he also honoured the champagne with equal attention.

We spent three hours at the table and then proceeded to the third floor, where Sophie accompanied her mother's singing on the piano, and young Cornelis displayed his flute-playing talents. Mr. Steyne swore that he had never been present at such a pleasant party in his life, adding that pleasure was forbidden fruit in England on Sundays and holidays. This convinced me that Steyne was an intelligent man, though his French was execrable. He left at seven, after giving a beautiful ring to my daughter, whom he escorted back to school with Miss Nancy.

The Marquis Petina foolishly observed to me that he did not know where to find a bed. I understood what he wanted, but I told him he would easily find one with a little money. Taking his sweetheart aside I gave her a guinea for him, begging her to tell him not to visit me again till he was invited.

When all the guests were gone, I led the five sisters to the mother's room. She was wonderfully well, eating, drinking, and sleeping to admiration, and never doing anything, not even reading or writing. She enjoyed the 'dolce far niente' in all the force of the term. However, she told me she was always thinking of her family, and of the laws which it imposed on her.

I could scarcely help laughing, but I only said that if these laws were the same as those which her charming daughters followed, I thought them wiser than Solon's.

I drew Augusta on to my knee, and said,—

"My lady, allow me to kiss your delightful daughter."

Instead of giving me a direct answer, the old hypocrite began a long sermon on the lawfulness of the parental kiss. All the time Augusta was lavishing on me secret but delicious endearments.

'O tempora! O mores!'

The next day I was standing at my window, when the Marquis Caraccioli, who was passing by, greeted me, and asked me if he could come in. I bade him welcome, and summoning the eldest sister told the ambassador that this young lady was going to marry the Marquis Petina as soon as his remittances arrived.

He addressed himself to her, and spoke as follows:

"Mademoiselle, it is true that your lover is really a marquis, but he is very poor and will never have any money; and if he goes back to Naples he will be imprisoned, and if he is released from the State prison his creditors will put him in the Vittoria."

However this salutary warning had no effect.

After the ambassador had taken his leave I was dressing to take a ride when Augusta told me that, if I liked, Hippolyta her sister would come with me, as she could ride beautifully.

"That's amusing," said I, "make her come down."

Hippolyta came down and begged me to let her ride with me, saying that she would do me credit.

"Certainly;" said I, "but have you a man's riding suit or a woman's costume?"

"No."

"Then we must put off the excursion till to-morrow."

I spent the day in seeing that a suit was made for her, and I felt quite amorous when Pegu, the tailor, measured her for the breeches. Everything was done in time and we had a charming ride, for she managed her horse with wonderful skill.

After an excellent supper, to which wine had not been lacking, the happy Hippolyta accompanied Victoire into my room and helped her to undress. When she kissed her sister I asked if she would not give me a kiss too, and after some jesting Augusta changed the joke into earnest by bidding her come to bed beside me, without taking the trouble to ask my leave, so sure did she feel of my consent. The night was well spent, and I had no reason to complain of want of material, but Augusta wisely let the newcomer have the lion's share of my attentions.

Next day we rode out again in the afternoon, followed by my negro, who was a skilful horseman himself. In Richmond Park Hippolyta's dexterity astonished me; she drew all eyes on her. In the evening we came home well pleased with our day's ride, and had a good supper.

As the meal proceeded I noticed that Gabrielle, the youngest of all, looked sad and a little sulky. I asked her the reason, and with a little pout that became her childish face admirably, she replied,—

"Because I can ride on horseback as well as my sister."

"Very good," said I, "then you shall ride the day after to-morrow." This put her into a good temper again.

Speaking of Hippolyta's skill, I asked her where she had learnt to ride. She simply burst out laughing. I asked her why she laughed, and she said,—

"Why, because I never learnt anywhere; my only masters were courage and some natural skill."

"And has your sister learnt?"

"No," said Gabrielle, "but I can ride just as well."

I could scarcely believe it, for Hippolyta had seemed to float on her horse, and her riding skewed the utmost skill and experience. Hoping that her sister would vie with her, I said that I would take them out together, and the very idea made them both jump with joy.

Gabrielle was only fifteen, and her shape, though not fully developed, was well marked, and promised a perfect beauty by the time she was in her maturity. Full of grace and simplicity, she said she would like to come with me to my room, and I readily accepted her offer, not caring whether the scheme had been concerted between her and her other sisters.

As soon as we were alone, she told me that she had never had a lover, and she allowed me to assure myself of the fact with the same child-like simplicity. Gabrielle was like all the others; I would have chosen her if I had been obliged to make the choice. She made me feel sorry for her sake, to hear that the mother had made up her mind to leave. In the morning I gave her her fee of twenty guineas and a handsome ring as a mark of my peculiar friendship, and we spent the day in getting ready our habits for the ride of the day following.

Gabrielle got on horseback as if she had had two years in the riding school. We went along the streets at a walking pace, but as soon as we were in the open country we broke into a furious gallop, and kept it up till we got to Barnet, where we stopped to breakfast. We had done the journey in twenty-five minutes, although the distance is nearly ten miles. This may seem incredible, but the English horses are wonderfully swift, and we were all of us well mounted. My two nymphs looked ravishing. I adored them, and I adored myself for making them so happy.

Just as we were remounting, who should arrive but Lord Pembroke. He was on his way to St. Alban's. He stopped his horse, and admired the graceful riding of my two companions; and not recognizing them immediately, he begged leave to pay his court to them. How I laughed to myself! At last he recognized them, and congratulated me on my conquest, asking if I loved Hippolyta. I guessed his meaning, and said I only loved Gabrielle.

"Very good," said he; "may I come and see you?"

"Certainly," I replied.

After a friendly hand-shake we set out once more, and were soon back   in London.

Gabrielle was done up and went to bed directly; she slept on till the next morning without my disturbing her peaceful sleep, and when she awoke and found herself in my arms, she began to philosophise.

"How easy it is," said she, "to be happy when one is rich, and how sad it is to see happiness out of one's reach for lack of a little money. Yesterday I was the happiest of beings, and why should I not be as happy all my days? I would gladly agree that my life should be short provided that it should be a happy one."

I, too, philosophised, but my reflections were sombre. I saw my resources all but exhausted, and I began to meditate a journey to

Lisbon. If my fortune had been inexhaustible, the Hanoverians might have held me in their silken fetters to the end of my days. It seemed to me as if I loved them more like a father than a lover, and the fact that I slept with them only added to the tenderness of the tie. I looked into Gabrielle's eyes, and there I saw but love. How could such a love exist in her unless she were naturally virtuous, and yet devoid of those prejudices which are instilled into us in our early years.

The next day Pembroke called and asked me to give him a dinner. Augusta delighted him. He made proposals to her which excited her laughter as he did not want to pay till after the event, and she would not admit this condition. However, he gave her a bank note for ten guineas before he left, and she accepted it with much grace. The day after he wrote her a letter, of which I shall speak presently.

A few minutes after the nobleman had gone the mother sent for me to come to her, and after paying an eloquent tribute to my virtues, my generosity, and my unceasing kindness towards her family, she made the following proposal:

"As I feel sure that you have all the love of a father for my daughters, I wish you to become their father in reality! I offer you my hand and heart; become my husband, you will be their father, their lord and mine. What do you say to this?"

I bit my lips hard and had great difficulty in restraining my inclination to laughter. Nevertheless, the amazement, the contempt, and the indignation which this unparalleled piece of impudence aroused in me soon brought me to myself. I perceived that this consummate hypocrite had counted on an abrupt refusal, and had only made this ridiculous offer with the idea of convincing me that she was under the impression that I had left her daughters as I had found them, and that the money I had spent on them was merely a sign of my tender and fatherly affection. Of course she knew perfectly well how the land lay, but she thought to justify herself by taking this step. She was aware that I could only look upon such a proposal as an insult, but she did not care for that.

I resolved to keep on the mask, and replied that her proposition was undoubtedly a very great honour for me, but it was also a very important question, and so I begged her to allow me some time for consideration.

When I got back to my room I found there the mistress of the wretched Marquis Petina, who told me that her happiness depended on a certificate from the Neapolitan ambassador that her lover was really the person he professed to be. With this document he would be able to claim a sum of two hundred guineas, and then they could both go to Naples, and he would marry her there. "He will easily obtain the royal pardon," said she. "You, and you alone, can help us in the matter, and I commend myself to your kindness."

I promised to do all I could for her. In fact, I called on the ambassador, who made no difficulty about giving the required certificate. For the moment my chilly conquest was perfectly happy, but though I saw she was very grateful to me I did not ask her to prove her gratitude.

CHAPTER XVI

Augusta Becomes Lord Pembroke's Titular Mistress The King of Corsica's Son—M. du Claude, or the Jesuit Lavalette—Departure of the Hanoverians I Balance My Accounts—The Baron Stenau—The English Girl, and What She Gave Me—Daturi—My Flight from London—Comte St. Germain—Wesel

Lord Pembroke wrote to Augusta offering her fifty guineas a month for three years, with lodging, board, servants, and carriage at St. Albans, without reckoning what she might expect from his grateful affection if it were returned.

Augusta translated the letter for me, and asked for my advice.

"I can't give you any counsel," said I, "in a matter which only concerns your own heart and your own interests."

She went up to her mother, who would come to no conclusion without first consulting me, because, as she said, I was the wisest and most virtuous of men. I am afraid the reader will differ from her here, but I comfort myself by the thought that I, too, think like the reader. At last it was agreed that Augusta should accept the offer if Lord Pembroke would find a surety in the person of some reputable London merchant, for with her beauty and numerous graces she was sure to, become Lady Pembroke before long. Indeed, the mother said she was perfectly certain of it, as otherwise she could not have given her consent, as her daughters were countesses, and too good to be any man's mistresses.

The consequence was that Augusta wrote my lord a letter, and in three days it was all settled. The merchant duly signed the contract, at the foot of which I had the honour of inscribing my name as a witness, and then I took the merchant to the mother, and he witnessed her cession of her daughter. She would not see Pembroke, but she kissed her daughter, and held a private colloquy with her.

The day on which Augusta left my house was signalized by an event which I must set down.

The day after I had given the Marquis Petina's future bride the required certificate, I had taken out Gabrielle and Hippolyta for a ride. When I got home I found waiting for me a person calling himself Sir Frederick, who was said to be the son of Theodore, King of Corsica, who had died in London. This gentleman said he wished to speak to me in private, and when we were alone he said he was aware of my acquaintance with the Marquis Petina, and being on the eve of discounting a bill of two hundred guineas for him he wished to be informed whether it was likely that he could meet the bill when it fell due.

"It is important that I should be informed on that point," he added, "for the persons who are going to discount the bill want me to put my signature to it."

"Sir," I replied, "I certainly am acquainted with the marquis, but I know nothing about his fortune. However, the Neapolitan ambassador assured me that he was the Marquis Petina."

"If the persons who have the matter in hand should drop it, would you discount the bill? You shall have it cheap."

"I never meddle with these speculations. Good day, Sir Frederick."

The next day Goudar came and said that a M. du Claude wanted to speak to me.

"Who is M. du Claude?"

"The famous Jesuit Lavalette, who was concerned in the great bankruptcy case which ruined the Society in France. He fled to England under a false name. I advise you to listen to him, for he must have plenty of money."

"A Jesuit and a bankrupt; that does not sound very well."

"Well, I have met him in good houses, and knowing that I was acquainted with you he addressed himself to me. After all, you run no risk in listening to what he has to say."

"Well, well, you can take me to him; it will be easier to avoid any entanglement than if he came to see me."

Goudar went to Lavalette to prepare the way, and in the afternoon he took me to see him. I was well enough pleased to see the man, whose rascality had destroyed the infamous work of many years. He welcomed me with great politeness, and as soon as we were alone he shewed me a bill of Petina's, saying,—

"The young man wants me to discount it, and says you can give me the necessary information."

I gave the reverend father the same answer as I had given the King of Corsica's son, and left him angry with this Marquis of Misery who had given me so much needless trouble. I was minded to have done with him, and resolved to let him know through his mistress that I would not be his reference, but I could not find an opportunity that day.

The next day I took my two nymphs for a ride, and asked Pembroke to dinner. In vain we waited for Petina's mistress; she was nowhere to be found. At nine o'clock I got a letter from her, with a German letter enclosed for her mother. She said that feeling certain that her mother would not give her consent to her marriage, she had eloped with her lover, who had got together enough money to go to Naples, and when they reached that town he would marry her. She begged me to console her mother and make her listen to reason, as she had not gone off with an adventurer but with a man of rank, her equal. My lips curled into a smile of pity and contempt, which made the three sisters curious. I shewed them the letter I had just received, and asked them to come with me to their mother.

"Not to-night," said Victoire, "this terrible news would keep her awake."

I took her advice and we supped together, sadly enough.

I thought the poor wretch was ruined for life, and I reproached myself with being the cause of her misfortune; for if I had not released the marquis from prison this could never have happened. The Marquis Caraccioli had been right in saying that I had done a good deed, but a foolish one. I consoled myself in the arms of my dear Gabrielle.

I had a painful scene with the mother the next morning. She cursed her daughter and her seducer, and even blamed me. She wept and stormed alternately.

It is never of any use to try and convince people in distress that they are wrong, for one may only do harm, while if they are left to themselves they soon feel that they have been unjust, and are grateful to the person who let them exhaust their grief without any contradiction.

After this event I spent a happy fortnight in the society of Gabrielle, whom Hippolyta and Victoire looked on as my wife. She made my happiness and I made hers in all sorts of ways, but especially by my fidelity; for I treated her sisters as if they had been my sisters, shewing no recollection of the favours I had obtained from them, and never taking the slightest liberty, for I knew that friendship between women will hardly brook amorous rivalry. I had bought them dresses and linen in abundance, they were well lodged and well fed, I took them to the theatre and to the country, and the consequence was they all adored me, and seemed to think that this manner of living would go on for ever. Nevertheless, I was every day nearer and nearer to moral and physical bankruptcy. I had no more money, and I had sold all my diamonds and precious stones. I still possessed my snuff-boxes, my watches, and numerous trifles, which I loved and had not the heart to sell; and, indeed, I should not have got the fifth part of what I gave for them. For a whole month I had not paid my cook, or my wine merchant, but I liked to feel that they trusted me. All I thought of was Gabrielle's love, and of this I assured myself by a thousand delicacies and attentions.

This was my condition when one day Victoire came to me with sadness on her face, and said that her mother had made up her mind to return to Hanover, as she had lost all hope of getting anything from the English Court.

"When does she intend to leave?"

"In three or four days."

"And is she going without telling me, as if she were leaving an inn after paying her bill?"

"On the contrary, she wishes to have a private talk with you."

I paid her a visit, and she began by reproaching me tenderly for not coming to see her more often. She said that as I had refused her hand she would not run the risk of incurring censure or slander of any kind. "I thank you from my heart," she added, "for all the kindness you have shewn my girls, and I am going to take the three I have left away, lest I lose them as I have lost the two eldest. If you like, you may come too and stay with us as long as you like in my pretty country house near the capital."

Of course I had to thank her and reply that my engagements did not allow me to accept her kind offer.

Three days after, Victoire told me, as I was getting up, that they were going on board ship at three o'clock. Hippolyta and Gabrielle made me come for a ride, according to a promise I had given them the night before. The poor things amused themselves, while I grieved bitterly, as was my habit when I had to separate from anyone that I loved.

When we came home I lay down on my bed, not taking any dinner, and seeing nothing of the three sisters till they had made everything ready for the journey. I got up directly before they left, so as not to see the mother in my own room, and I saw her in hers just as she was about to be taken down into my carriage, which was in readiness at the door. The impudent creature expected me to give her some money for the journey, but perceiving that I was not likely to bleed, she observed, with involuntary sincerity, that her purse contained the sum of a hundred and fifty guineas, which I had given to her daughters; and these daughters of hers were present, and sobbed bitterly.

When they were gone I closed my doors to everyone, and spent three days in the melancholy occupation of making up my accounts. In the month I had spent with the Hanoverians I had dissipated the whole of the sum resulting from the sale of the precious stones, and I found that I was in debt to the amount of four hundred guineas. I resolved to go to Lisbon by sea, and sold my diamond cross, six or seven gold snuff-boxes (after removing the portraits), all my watches except one, and two great trunks full of clothes. I then discharged my debts and found I was eighty guineas to the good, this being what remained of the fine fortune I had squandered away like a fool or a philosopher, or, perhaps, a little like both. I left my fine house where I had lived so pleasantly, and took a little room at a guinea a week. I still kept my negro, as I had every reason to believe him to be a faithful servant.

After taking these measures I wrote to M. de Bragadin, begging him to send me two hundred sequins.

Thus having made up my mind to leave London without owing a penny to anyone, and under obligations to no man's purse, I waited for the bill of exchange from Venice. When it came I resolved to bid farewell to all my friends and to try my fortune in Lisbon, but such was not the fate which the fickle goddess had assigned to me.

A fortnight after the departure of the Hanoverians (it was the end of February in the year 1764), my evil genius made me go to the "Canon Tavern," where I usually dined in a room by myself. The table was laid and I was just going to sit down, when Baron Stenau came in and begged me to have my dinner brought into the next room, where he and his mistress were dining.

"I thank you," said I, "for the solitary man grows weary of his company."

I saw the English woman I had met at Sartori's, the same to whom the baron had been so generous. She spoke Italian, and was attractive in many ways, so I was well pleased to find myself opposite to her, and we had a pleasant dinner.

After a fortnight's abstinence it was not surprising that she inspired me with desires, but I concealed them nevertheless, for her lover seemed to respect her. I only allowed myself to tell the baron that I thought him the happiest of men.

Towards the close of the dinner the girl noticed three dice on the mantel and took them up, saying,—

"Let us have a wager of a guinea, and spend it on oysters and champagne."

We could not refuse, and the baron having lost called the waiter and gave him his orders.

While we were eating the oysters she suggested that we should throw again to see which should pay for the dinner.

We did so and she lost.

I did not like my luck, and wishing to lose a couple of guineas I offered to throw against the baron. He accepted, and to my annoyance I won. He asked for his revenge and lost again.

"I don't want to win your money," said I, "and I will give you your revenge up to a hundred guineas."

He seemed grateful and we went on playing, and in less than half an hour he owed me a hundred guineas.

"Let us go on," said he.

"My dear baron, the luck's against you; you might lose a large sum of money. I really think we have had enough."

Without heeding my politeness, he swore against fortune and against the favour I seemed to be shewing him. Finally he got up, and taking his hat and cane, went out, saying,—

"I will pay you when I come back."

As soon as he had gone the girl said:

"I am sure you have been regarding me as your partner at play."

"If you have guessed that, you will also have guessed that I think you charming."

"Yes, I think I have."

"Are you angry with me?"

"Not in the least."

"You shall have the fifty guineas as soon as he has paid me."

"Very good, but the baron must know nothing about it."

"Of course not."

The bargain was scarcely struck before I began to shew her how much I loved her. I had every reason to congratulate myself on her complaisance, and I thought this meeting a welcome gleam of light when all looked dark around me. We had to make haste, however, as the door was only shut with a catch. I had barely time to ascertain her address and the hour at which she could see me, and whether I should have to be careful with her lover. She replied that the baron's fidelity was not of a character to make him very exacting. I put the address in my pocket, and promised to pass a night with her.

The baron came in again, and said,—

"I have been to a merchant to discount this bill of exchange, and though it is drawn on one of the best house in Cadiz, and made out by a good house in London, he would not have anything to do with it."

I took the bill and saw some millions mentioned on it, which astonished me.

The baron said with a laugh that the currency was Portuguese milries, and that they amounted to five hundred pounds sterling.

"If the signatures are known," said I, "I don't understand why the man won't discount it. Why don't you take it to your banker?"

"I haven't got one. I came to England with a thousand gold pieces in my pocket, and I have spent them all. As I have not got any letters of credit I cannot pay you unless the bill is discounted. If you have got any friends on the Exchange, however, you could get it done."

"If the names prove good ones I will let you have the money to-morrow morning."

"Then I will make it payable to your order."

He put his name to it, and I promised to send him either the money or the bill before noon on the day following. He gave me his address and begged me to come and dine with him, and so we parted.

The next day I went to Bosanquet, who told me that Mr. Leigh was looking out for bills of exchange on Cadiz, and I accordingly waited on him. He exclaimed that such paper was worth more than gold to him, and gave me five hundred and twenty guineas, of course after I had endorsed it.

I called on the baron and gave him the money I had just received, and he thanked me and gave me back the hundred guineas. Afterwards we had dinner, and fell to talking of his mistress.

"Are you in love with her?" said I.

"No; I have plenty of others, and if you like her you can have her for ten guineas."

I liked this way of putting it, though I had not the slightest idea of cheating the girl out of the sum I had promised her. On leaving the baron I went to see her, and as soon as she heard that the baron had paid me she ordered a delicious supper, and made me spend a night that obliterated all my sorrows from my memory. In the morning, when I handed over the fifty guineas, she said that as a reward for the way in which I kept my promise I could sup with her whenever I liked to spend six guineas. I promised to come and see her often.

The next morning I received a letter through the post, written in bad Italian, and signed, "Your obedient godson, Daturi." This godson of mine was in prison for debt, and begged me to give him a few shillings to buy some food.

I had nothing particular to do, the appellation of godson made me curious, and so I went to the prison to see Daturi, of whose identity I had not the slightest idea. He was a fine young man of twenty; he did not know me, nor I him. I gave him his letter, and begging me to forgive him he drew a paper from his pocket and shewed me his certificate of baptism, on which I saw my own name inscribed beside his name and those of his father and mother, the parish of Venice, where he was born, and the church in which he was baptized; but still I racked my memory in vain; I could not recollect him.

"If you will listen to me," he said, "I can set you right; my mother has told me the story a hundred times."

"Go on," said I, "I will listen;" and as he told his story I remembered who he was.

This young man whom I had held at the font as the son of the actor Daturi was possibly my own son. He had come to London with a troupe of jugglers to play the illustrious part of clown, or pagliazzo, but having quarrelled with the company he had lost his place and had got into debt to the extent of ten pounds sterling, and for this debt he had been imprisoned. Without saying anything to him about my relations with his mother, I set him free on the spot, telling him to come to me every morning, as I would give him two shillings a day for his support.

A week after I had done this good work I felt that I had caught the fearful disease from which the god Mercury had already delivered me three times, though with great danger and peril of my life. I had spent three nights with the fatal English woman, and the misfortune was doubly inconvenient under the circumstances. I was on the eve of a long sea voyage, and though Venus may have risen from the waves of the sea, sea air is by no means favourable to those on whom she has cast her malign aspect. I knew what to do, and resolved to have my case taken in hand without delay.

I left my house, not with the intention of reproaching the English woman after the manner of fools, but rather of going to a good surgeon, with whom I could make an agreement to stay in his house till my cure was completed.

I had my trunks packed just as if I was going to leave London, excepting my linen, which I sent to my washerwoman who lived at a distance of six miles from town, and drove a great trade.

The very day I meant to change my lodging a letter was handed to me. It was from Mr. Leigh, and ran as follows:

"The bill of exchange I discounted for you is a forgery, so please to send me at your earliest convenience the five hundred and twenty guineas; and if the man who has cheated you will not reimburse the money, have him arrested. For Heaven's sake do not force me to have you arrested to-morrow, and whatever you do make haste, for this may prove a hanging matter."

Fortunately I was by myself when I received the letter. I fell upon my bed, and in a moment I was covered with a cold sweat, while I trembled like a leaf. I saw the gallows before me, for nobody would lend me the money, and they would not wait for my remittance from Venice to reach me.

To my shuddering fit succeeded a burning fever. I loaded my pistols, and went out with the determination of blowing out Baron Stenau's brains, or putting him under arrest if he did not give me the money. I reached his house, and was informed that he had sailed for Lisbon four days ago.

This Baron Stenau was a Livonian, and four months after these events he was hanged at Lisbon. I only anticipate this little event in his life because I might possibly forget it when I come to my sojourn at Riga.

As soon as I heard he was gone I saw there was no remedy, and that I must save myself. I had only ten or twelve guineas left, and this sum was insufficient. I went to Treves, a Venetian Jew to whom I had a letter from Count Algarotti, the Venetian banker. I did not think of going to Bosanquet, or Sanhel, or Salvador, who might possibly have got wind of my trouble, while Treves had no dealings with these great bankers, and discounted a bill for a hundred sequins readily enough. With the money in my pocket I made my way to my lodging, while deadly fear dogged every step. Leigh had given me twenty-four hours' breathing time, and I did not think him capable of breaking his word, still it would not do to trust to it. I did not want to lose my linen nor three fine suits of clothes which my tailor was keeping for me, and yet I had need of the greatest promptitude.

I called in Jarbe and asked him whether he would prefer to take twenty guineas and his dismissal, or to continue in my service. I explained that he would have to wait in London for a week, and join me at the place from which I wrote to him.

"Sir," said he, "I should like to remain in your service, and I will rejoin you wherever you please. When are you leaving?"

"In an hour's time; but say not a word, or it will cost me my life."

"Why can't you take me with you?"

"Because I want you to bring my linen which is at the wash, and my clothes which the tailor is making. I will give you sufficient money for the journey."

"I don't want anything. You shall pay me what I have spent when I rejoin you. Wait a moment."

He went out and came back again directly, and holding out sixty guineas, said,—

"Take this, sir, I entreat you, my credit is good for as much more in case of need."

"I thank you, my good fellow, but I will not take your money, but be sure I will not forget your fidelity."

My tailor lived close by and I called on him, and seeing that my clothes were not yet made up I told him that I should like to sell them, and also the gold lace that was to be used in the trimming. He instantly gave me thirty guineas which meant a gain to him of twenty-five per cent. I paid the week's rent of my lodging, and after bidding farewell to my negro I set out with Daturi. We slept at Rochester, as my strength would carry me no farther. I was in convulsions, and had a sort of delirium. Daturi was the means of saving my life.

I had ordered post-horses to continue our journey, and Daturi of his own authority sent them back and went for a doctor, who pronounced me to be in danger of an apoplectic fit and ordered a copious blood-letting, which restored my calm. Six hours later he pronounced me fit to travel. I got to Dover early in the morning, and had only half an hour to stop, as the captain of the packet said that the tide would not allow of any delay. The worthy sailor little knew how well his views suited mine. I used this half hour in writing to Jarbe, telling him to rejoin me at Calais, and Mrs. Mercier, my landlady, to whom I had addressed the letter, wrote to tell me that she had given it him with her own hands. However, Jarbe did not come. We shall hear more of this negro in the course of two years.

The fever and the virus that was in my blood put me in danger of my life, and on the third day I was in extremis. A fourth blood-letting exhausted my strength, and left me in a state of coma which lasted for twenty-four hours. This was succeeded by a crisis which restored me to life again, but it was only by dint of the most careful treatment that I found myself able to continue my journey a fortnight after my arrival in France.

Weak in health, grieved at having been the innocent cause of the worthy

Mr. Leigh's losing a large sum of money, humiliated by my flight from London, indignant with Jarbe, and angry at being obliged to abandon my Portuguese project, I got into a post-chaise with Daturi, not knowing where to turn or where to go, or whether I had many more weeks to live.

I had written to Venice asking M. de Bragadin to send the sum I have mentioned to Brussels instead of London.

When I got to Dunkirk, the day after I left Paris, the first person I saw was the merchant S——, the husband of that Therese whom my readers may remember, the niece of Tiretta's mistress, with whom I had been in love seven years ago. The worthy man recognized me, and seeing his astonishment at the change in my appearance I told him I was recovering from a long illness, and then asked after his wife.

"She is wonderfully well," he answered, "and I hope we shall have the pleasure of seeing you to dinner tomorrow."

I said I wanted to be off at day-break, but he would not hear of it, and protested he would be quite hurt if I went away without seeing his wife and his three children. At last I appeased him by saying that we would sup together.

My readers will remember that I had been on the point of marrying Therese, and this circumstance made me ashamed of presenting myself to her in such a sorry plight.

In a quarter of an hour the husband arrived with his wife and three children, the eldest of whom looked, about six. After the usual greetings and tiresome enquiries after my health, Therese sent back the two younger children, rightly thinking that the eldest would be the only one in whom I should take any interest. He was a charming boy; and as he was exactly like his mother, the worthy merchant had no doubts as to the parentage of the child.

I laughed to myself at finding my offspring thus scattered all over Europe. At supper Therese gave me news of Tiretta. He had entered the Dutch East India Company's service, but having been concerned in a revolt at Batavia, he had only escaped the gallows by flight—I had my own thoughts as to the similarity between his destiny and mine, but I did not reveal them. After all it is an easy enough matter for an adventurous man, who does not look where he is going, to get hanged for a mere trifle.

The next day, when I got to Tournay, I saw some grooms walking fine horses up and down, and I asked to whom they belonged.

"To the Comte de St. Germain, the adept, who has been here a month, and never goes out. Everybody who passes through the place wants to see him; but he is invisible."

This was enough to give me the same desire, so I wrote him a letter, expressing my wish to speak to him, and asking him to name an hour. His reply, which I have preserved, ran as follows:

"The gravity of my occupation compels me to exclude everyone, but you are an exception. Come whenever you like, you will be shewn in. You need not mention my name nor your own. I do not ask you to share my repast, for my food is not suitable to others—to you least of all, if your appetite is what it used to be."

At nine o'clock I paid my call, and found he had grown a beard two inches long. He had a score of retorts before him, full of liquids in various stages of digestion. He told me he was experimenting with colours for his own amusement, and that he had established a hat factory for Count Cobenzl, the Austrian ambassador at Brussels. He added that the count had only given him a hundred and fifty thousand florins, which were insufficient. Then we spoke of Madame d'Urfe.

"She poisoned herself," said he, "by taking too strong a dose of the Universal Medicine, and her will shews that she thought herself to be with child. If she had come to me, I could have really made her so, though it is a difficult process, and science has not advanced far enough for us to be able to guarantee the sex of the child."

When he heard the nature of my disease, he wanted me to stay three days at Tournay for him to give me fifteen pills, which would effectually cure me, and restore me to perfect health. Then he shewed me his magistrum, which he called athoeter. It was a white liquid contained in a well-stoppered phial. He told me that this liquid was the universal spirit of nature, and that if the wax on the stopper was pricked ever so lightly, the whole of the contents would disappear. I begged him to make the experiment. He gave me the phial and a pin, and I pricked the wax, and to lo! the phial was empty.

"It is very fine," said I, "but what good is all this?"

"I cannot tell you; that is my secret."

He wanted to astonish me before I went, and asked me if I had any money about me. I took out several pieces and put them on the table. He got up, and without saying what he was going to do he took a burning coal and put it on a metal plate, and placed a twelve-sols piece with a small black grain on the coal. He then blew it, and in two minutes it seemed on fire.

"Wait a moment," said the alchemist, "let it get cool;" and it cooled almost directly.

"Take it; it is yours," said he.

I took up the piece of money and found it had become gold. I felt perfectly certain that he had smuggled my silver piece away, and had substituted a gold piece coated with silver for it. I did not care to tell him as much, but to let him see that I was not taken in, I said,—

"It is really very wonderful, but another time you should warn me what you are going to do, so that the operation might be attentively watched, and the piece of money noted before being placed on the burning coal."

"Those that are capable of entertaining doubts of my art," said the rogue, "are not worthy to speak to me."

This was in his usual style of arrogance, to which I was accustomed. This was the last time I saw this celebrated and learned impostor; he died at Schlesing six or seven years after. The piece of money he gave me was pure gold, and two months after Field-marshal Keith took such a fancy to it that I gave it him.

I left Tournay the next morning, and stopped at Brussels to await the answer of the letter which I had written to M. de Bragadin. Five days after I got the letter with a bill of exchange for two hundred ducats.

I thought of staying in Brussels to get cured, but Daturi told me that he had heard from a rope-dancer that his father and mother and the whole family were at Brunswick, and he persuaded me to go there, assuring me that I should be carefully looked after.

He had not much difficulty in getting me to go to Brunswick, as I was curious to see again the mother of my godson, so I started the same day. At Ruremonde I was so ill that I had to stop for thirty-six hours. At Wesel I wished to get rid of my post-chaise, for the horses of the country are not used to going between shafts, but what was my surprise to meet General Bekw there.

After the usual compliments had passed, and the general had condoled with me on my weak state of health, he said he should like to buy my chaise and exchange it for a commodious carriage, in which I could travel all over Germany. The bargain was soon struck, and the general advised me to stay at Wesel where there was a clever young doctor from the University of Leyden, who would understand my case better than the Brunswick physicians.

Nothing is easier than to influence a sick man, especially if he be in search of fortune, and knows not where to look for the fickle goddess. General Bekw——, who was in garrison at Wesel, sent for Dr. Pipers, and was present at my confession and even at the examination.

I will not revolt my readers by describing the disgusting state in which
I was, suffice it to say that I shudder still when I think of it.

The young doctor, who was gentleness personified, begged me to come and stay with him, promising that his mother and sisters should take the greatest care of me, and that he would effect a radical cure in the course of six weeks if I would carry out all his directions. The general advised me strongly to stay with the doctor, and I agreed all the more readily as I wished to have some amusement at Brunswick and not to arrive there deprived of the use of all my limbs. I therefore gave in, but the doctor would not hear of any agreement. He told me that I could give him whatever I liked when I went away, and he would certainly be satisfied. He took his leave to go and make my room ready, and told me to come in an hour's time. I went to his house in a sedan-chair, and held a handkerchief before my face, as I was ashamed that the young doctor's mother and sisters should see me in the state I was in.

As soon as I got to my room, Daturi undressed me and I went to bed.

CHAPTER XVII

My Cure—Daturi is Beaten by Some Soldiers—I Leave Wesel for Brunswick—Redegonde—Brunswick—The Hereditary Prince—The Jew—My Stay at Wolfen-Buttel The Library—Berlin Calsabigi and the Berlin Lottery—Mdlle. Belanger

At Supper-time, the doctor, his mother, and one of his sisters came to see me. All of them bore the love of their kind written on their features; they assured me that I should have all possible care at their hands. When the ladies were gone the doctor explained his treatment. He said that he hoped to cure me by the exhibition of sudorifices and mercurial pills, but he warned me I must be very careful in my diet and must not apply myself in any way. I promised to abide by his directions, and he said that he would read me the newspaper himself twice a week to amuse me, and by way of a beginning he informed me that the famous Pompadour was dead.

Thus I was condemned to a state of perfect rest, but it was not the remedies or the abstinence I dreaded most; I feared the effects of ennui; I thought I should die of it. No doubt the doctor saw the danger as well as myself, for he asked me if I would mind his sister coming and working in my room occasionally with a few of her friends. I replied that, despite my shame of shewing myself to young ladies in such a condition, I accepted her offer with delight. The sister was very grateful for what she was pleased to call my kindness, for my room was the only one which looked in the street, and as everyone knows girls are very fond of inspecting the passers-by. Unfortunately this arrangement turned out ill for

Daturi. The poor young man had only received the education of a mountebank, and it was tiresome for him to pass all his time in my company. When he saw that I had plenty of friends, he thought I could dispense with his society, and only thought of amusing himself. On the third day towards the evening he was carried home covered with bruises. He had been in the guard-room with the soldiers, and some quarrel having arisen he had got a severe beating. He was in a pitiable state; all over blood and with three teeth missing. He told me the story with tears, and begged me to take vengeance on his foes.

I sent my doctor to General Bekw——, who said that all he could do was to give the poor man a bed in the hospital. Baturi had no bones broken, and in a few days was quite well, so I sent him on to Brunswick with a passport from General Salomon. The loss of his teeth secured him from the conscription; this, at any rate, was a good thing.

The treatment of the young doctor was even more successful than he had anticipated, for in a month I was perfectly well again, though terribly thin. The worthy people of the house must have taken an idea of me not in the least like myself; I was thought to be the most patient of men, and the sister and her young lady friends must have considered me as modesty personified; but these virtues only resulted from my illness and my great depression. If you want to discover the character of a man, view him in health and freedom; a captive and in sickness he is no longer the same man.

I gave a beautiful dress to the sister, and twenty louis to the doctor, and both seemed to me extremely satisfied.

On the eve of my departure I received a letter from Madame du Rumain, who had heard I was in want from my friend Baletti, and sent me a bill of exchange on Amsterdam for six hundred florins. She said I could repay her at my convenience, but she died before I was able to discharge the debt.

Having made up my mind to go to Brunswick, I could not resist the temptation to pass through Hanover, for whenever I thought of Gabrielle I loved her still. I did not wish to stop any length of time, for I was poor and I had to be careful of my health. I only wished to pay her a flying visit on the estate which her mother had at Stocken, as she had told me. I may also say that curiosity was a motive for this visit.

I had decided to start at day-break in my new carriage, but the fates had ordained it otherwise.

The English general wrote me a note asking me to sup with him, telling me that some Italians would be present, and this decided me to stay on, but I had to promise the doctor to observe strict temperance.

My surprise may be imagined when I saw the Redegonde and her abominable mother. The mother did not recognize me at first, but Redegonde knew me directly, and said,—

"Good Heavens! how thin you have become!"

I complimented her on her beauty, and indeed she had improved wonderfully.

"I have just recovered from a dangerous illness," said I, "and I am starting for Brunswick at day-break tomorrow."

"So are we," she exclaimed, looking at her mother.

The general, delighted to find that we knew each other, said we could travel together.

"Hardly, I think," I replied, "unless the lady-mother has changed her principles since I knew her."

"I am always the same," she said, dryly enough; but I only replied with a glance of contempt.

The general held a bank at faro at a small table. There were several other ladies and some officers, and the stakes were small. He offered me a place, but I excused myself, saying that I never played while on a journey.

At the end of the deal the general returned to the charge, and said,—

"Really, chevalier, this maxim of yours is anti-social; you must play."

So saying he drew several English bank notes from his pocket-book, telling me they were the same I had given him in London six months ago.

"Take your revenge," he added; "there are four hundred pounds here."

"I don't want to lose as much as that," I replied, "but I will risk fifty pounds to amuse you."

With this I took out the bill of exchange that Madame du Rumain had sent me.

The general went on dealing, and at the third deal I found I was fifty guineas to the good, and with that I was satisfied. Directly afterwards supper was announced, and we went into the dining-room.

Redegonde, who had learnt French admirably, kept everybody amused. She had been engaged by the Duke of Brunswick as second singer, and she had come from Brussels. She bemoaned her journey in the uncomfortable post-chaise, and expressed a fear that she would be ill by the time she got to her journey's end.

"Why, there's the Chevalier Seingalt all alone in a most comfortable carriage," said the general.

Redegonde smiled.

"How many people will your carriage hold?"

"Only two."

"Then it's out of the question, for I never let my daughter travel alone with anybody."

A general burst of laughter, in which Redegonde joined, seemed to confuse the mother in some degree; but like a good daughter Redegonde explained that her mother was always afraid of her being assassinated.

The evening passed away in pleasant conversation, and the younger singer did not need much persuasion to seat herself at the piano, where she sang in a manner that won genuine applause.

When I wanted to go the general begged me to breakfast with him, saying that the post-chaise did not go till twelve, and that this act of politeness was due to my young fellow-countrywoman. Redegonde joined in, reproaching me with my behaviour at Turin and Florence, though she had nothing really to complain of. I gave in, and feeling that I wanted rest I went to bed.

The next morning, at nine o'clock, I took leave of the worthy doctor and his family and walked to the general's, giving orders that my carriage should be brought round as soon as it was ready.

In half an hour Redegonde and her mother arrived, and I was astonished to see them accompanied by the brother who had been my servant at Florence.

When breakfast was over my carriage stood at the door, and I made my bow to the general and all the company, who were standing in the hall to see me off. Redegonde came down the steps with me, and asked if my carriage was comfortable, and then got into it. I got in after her without the slightest premeditation, and the postillion, seeing the carriage full, gave a crack with his whip and we were off, Redegonde shrieking with laughter. I was on the point of telling him to stop, but seeing her enjoyment of the drive I held my tongue, only waiting for her to say, "I have had enough." But I waited in vain, and we had gone over half a league before she said a word.

"I have laughed, and laugh still," she said, "when I think of what my mother will say at this freak of mine. I had no intentions in getting into the carriage, and I am sure you cannot have told the postillion to drive on."

"You may be quite sure of that."

"All the same my mother will believe it to be a deeply-laid plan, and that strikes me as amusing."

"So it is; I am quite satisfied, certainly. Now you are here you had better come on with me to Brunswick; you will be more comfortable than in a villainous stage coach."

"I should be delighted, but that would be pushing matters too far. No, we will stop at the first stage and wait for the coach."

"You may do so if you please, but you will excuse my waiting."

"What! you would leave me all alone?"

"You know, dear Redegonde, that I have always loved you, and I am ready to take you with me to Brunswick; what more can I say?"

"If you love me you will wait with me and restore me to my mother, who must be in despair."

"In spite of my devotion I am afraid I cannot do so."

Instead of turning sulky the young madcap began to laugh again; and I determined she should come with me to Brunswick.

When we got to the end of the stage there were no horses ready. I arranged matters with the postillion, and after baiting the horses we set out once more. The roads were fearful, and we did not come to the second posting-stage till nightfall.

We might have slept there, but not wishing to be caught up by the coach and to lose my prize, I ordered fresh horses and we resumed our journey in spite of Redegonde's tears and supplications. We travelled all night and reached Lippstadt in the early morning, and in spite of the unseasonableness of the hour I ordered something to eat. Redegonde wanted a rest, as indeed did I, but she had to give way when I said caressingly that we could sleep at Minden. Instead of scolding me she began to smile, and I saw she guessed what she had to expect; in fact, when we got to Minden we had supper, and then went to bed together as man and wife, and stayed in bed for five hours. She was quite kind, and only made me entreat her for form's sake.

We got to Hanover and put up at an excellent inn where we had a choice meal, and where I found the waiter who was at the inn in Zurich when I waited on the ladies at table. Miss Chudleigh had dined there with the Duke of Kingston, and they had gone on to Berlin.

We had a beautiful French bed in which to spend the night, and in the morning we were awakened by the noise of the stage coach.

Redegonde not wishing to be surprised in my arms rang the bell and told the waiter by no means to admit the lady who would come out of the coach and ask to be shewn in directly; but her precaution was vain, for, as the waiter went out, the mother and son came in, and we were taken in 'flagrante delicto'.

I told them to wait outside, and getting up in my shirt I locked the door. The mother began to abuse me and her daughter, and threatened me with criminal proceedings if I did not give her up. Redegonde, however, calmed her by telling her the story, and she believed, or pretended to believe, it was all chance; but she said,—

"That's all very well; but you can't deny, you little slut, that you have been sleeping with him."

"Oh, there's no harm in that, for you know, dear mamma, nobody does anything asleep."

Without giving her the time to reply she threw her arms round her neck and promised to go on with her in the coach.

After things had been thus settled, I dressed myself, and gave them all a good breakfast, and went on my way to Brunswick, where I arrived a few hours before them.

Redegonde had deprived me of my curiosity to see Gabrielle; besides, in the condition I was in, my vanity would have suffered grievously. As soon as I had settled in a good inn I sent for Daturi, who came immediately, elegantly dressed, and very anxious to introduce to me a certain Signor Nicolini, theatrical manager. This Nicolini understood his craft perfectly, and was high in favour with the prince to whom his daughter Anna was mistress. He gave me a distinguished and a cordial greeting, and was very anxious that I should stay with him, but I was able to escape the constraint of such an arrangement without giving him any offense. I accepted his offer to take my meals at his table, which was furnished by an excellent cook and surrounded by a distinguished company. Here was no gathering of men of title, with the cold and haughty manners of the Court, all were talented, and such company to my mind was delightful.

I was not well, and I was not rich, or else I should have made a longer stay at Brunswick, which had its charms for me. But we will not anticipate, though as old age steals on a man he is never tired of dwelling again and again on the incidents of his past life, in spite of his desire to arrest the sands which run out so quickly.

The third day after my arrival at Brunswick, Redegonde knowing that I was dining at Nicolini's came there too. Everybody had found out, somehow or other, that we had travelled from Wesel to Hanover together, and they were at liberty to draw whatever conclusions they pleased.

Two days later the crown prince arrived from Potsdam on a visit to his future bride, the daughter of the reigning duke, whom he married the year after.

The Court entertained in the most magnificent manner, and the hereditary prince, now the reigning duke, honoured me with an invitation. I had met his highness at an assembly in Soho Square, the day after he had been made a London citizen.

It was twenty-two years since I had been in love with Daturi's mother. I was curious to see the ravages which time had worked on her, but I had reason to repent of my visit, for she had grown terribly ugly. She knew it herself, and a blush of shame appeared on those features which had once been fair.

The prince had an army of six thousand foot in good condition. This army was to be reviewed on a plain at a little distance from the town, and I went to see the spectacle, and was rewarded by having rain dripping down my back the whole time. Among the numerous spectators were many persons of fashion, ladies in handsome dresses, and a good sprinkling of foreigners. I saw the Honourable Miss Chudleigh, who honoured me by addressing me, and asked me, amongst other questions, how long I had left London. She was dressed in Indian muslin, and beneath it she only wore a chemise of fine cambric, and by the time the rain had made her clothes cling to her body she looked more than naked, but she did not evince any confusion. Most of the ladies sheltered themselves from the rain under elegant tents which had been erected.

The troops, who took no notice of the weather, executed their manoeuvres, and fired their muskets in a manner which seemed to satisfy good judges.

There was nothing further to attract me at Brunswick, and I thought of spending the summer at Berlin, which I concluded would be more amusing than a small provincial town. Wanting an overcoat I bought the material from a Jew, who offered to discount bills of exchange for me if I had any. I had the bill which

Madame du Rumain had sent me, and finding that it would be convenient for me to get it discounted, I gave it to the Israelite, who cashed it, deducting commission at the ordinary rate of two per cent. The letter was payable to the order of the Chevalier de Seingalt, and with that name I endorsed it.

I thought no more of the matter, but early the next day the same Jew called on me, and told me that I must either return him his money, or give sureties for the amount till he had ascertained whether the bill was a forgery or not.

I was offended at this piece of impertinence, and feeling certain that the bill was a good one I told the fellow that he might set his mind at rest and let me alone, as I should not give him any sureties.

"I must either have the money or the surety," said he, "and if you refuse I will have you arrested; your character is well known."

This was too much for me, and raising my cane I gave him a blow on the head which he must have felt for many a long day. I then dressed and dined with Nicolini, without thinking or speaking of this disagreeable incident.

The next day as I was taking a walk outside the town walls, I met the prince on horseback, followed by a single groom. I bowed to him as he passed, but he came up to me and said,—

"You are leaving Brunswick, chevalier?"

"In two or three days, your highness."

"I heard this morning that a Jew has brought a complaint against you for beating him because he asked you to give him security for a bill of exchange which he was afraid of."

"My lord, I cannot answer for the effects of my indignation against a rascal who dared to come and insult me in my own house, but I do know that if I had given him security I should have impugned my own honour. The impertinent scoundrel threatened to have me arrested, but I know that a just Government rules here, and not arbitrary power."

"You are right; it would be unjust to have you arrested, but he is afraid for his ducats."

"He need not be afraid, my lord, for the bill is drawn by a person of honour and of high station in society."

"I am delighted to hear it. The Jew said he would never have discounted the bill if you had not mentioned my name."

"That's a lie! Your highness' name never passed, my lips."

"He also says that you endorsed the bill with a false name."

"Then he lies again, for I signed myself Seingalt, and that name is mine."

"In short, it is a case of a Jew who has been beaten, and is afraid of being duped. I pity such an animal, and I must see what I can do to prevent his keeping you here till he learns the fate of the bill at Amsterdam. As I have not the slightest doubt as to the goodness of the bill, I will take it up myself, and this very morning: thus you will be able to leave when you like. Farewell, chevalier! I wish you a pleasant journey."

With this compliment the prince left me, without giving me time to answer him. I might have felt inclined to tell him that by taking up the bill he would give the Jew and everyone else to understand that it was a favour done to me, to the great hurt of my honour, and that consequently I should be obliged by his doing nothing of the kind. But though the prince was a man of generosity and magnanimity, he was deficient in that delicate quality which we call tact. This defect, common amongst princes, arises from their education, which places them above the politeness which is considered necessary in ordinary mortals.

He could not have treated me worse than he did, if he had been certain of my dishonesty, and wished me to understand that I was forgiven, and that he would bear all the consequences of my misdemeanour. With this idea in my head, I said to myself; "Perhaps, indeed, this is exactly what the prince does think. Is it the Jew or me that he pities? If the latter, I think I must give him a lesson, though I do not wish to cause him any humiliation."

Feeling deeply humiliated myself, and pondering on my position, I walked away, directing my attention especially to the duke's concluding words. I thought his wish for a pleasant journey supremely out of place, under the circumstances, in the mouth of one who enjoyed almost absolute power. It was equivalent to an order to leave the town, and I felt indignant at the thought.

I therefore resolved to vindicate my honour by neither going away nor remaining.

"If I stay," I said to myself, "the Jew will be adjudged to be in the right; and if I go the duke will think I have profited by his favour, and so to speak, by his present of fifty louis if the bill were protested. I will not let anyone enjoy a satisfaction which is no one due."

After these considerations, which I thought worthy of a wiser head than mine, I packed up my trunk, ordered horses, and after a good dinner and the payment of my bill I went to Wolfenbuttel with the idea of spending week there. I was sure of finding amusement, for Wolfenbuttel contains the third largest library in Europe, and I had long been anxious to see it.

The learned librarian, whose politeness was all the better for being completely devoid of affection, told me that not only could I have whatever books I wished to see, but that I could take them to my lodging, not even excepting the manuscripts, which are the chief feature in that fine library.

I spent a week in the library, only leaving it to take my meals and go to bed, and I count this week as one of the happiest I have ever spent, for then I forgot myself completely; and in the delight of study, the past, the present, and the future were entirely blotted out. Of some such sort, I think, must be the joys of the redeemed; and now I see that only a few trifling little circumstances and incidents were wanting to make me a perfect sage. And here I must note a circumstance which my readers may scarcely believe, but which, for all that, is quite true—namely, that I have always preferred virtue to vice, and that when I sinned I did so out of mere lightness of heart, for which, no doubt, I shall be blamed by many persons. But, no matter—a man has only to give an account of his actions to two beings, to himself here and to God hereafter.

At Wolfenbuttel I gathered a good many hints on the "Iliad" and "Odyssey," which will not be found in any commentator, and of which the great Pope knew nothing. Some of these considerations will be found in my translation of the "Iliad," the rest are still in manuscript, and will probably never see the light. However, I burn nothing, not even these Memoirs, though I often think of doing so, but the time never comes.

At the end of the week I returned to the same inn at Brunswick which I had occupied before, and let my godson Daturi know of my arrival.

I was delighted to hear that no one suspected that I had spent the fortnight within five leagues of Brunswick. Daturi told me that the general belief was that I had returned the Jew his money and got the bill of exchange back. Nevertheless I felt sure that the bill had been honoured at Amsterdam, and that the duke knew that I had been staying at Wolfenbuttel.

Daturi told me that Nicolini was expecting to see me at dinner, and I was not astonished to hear of it, for I had not taken leave of anyone. I accordingly went, and the following incident, which served to justify me in the eyes of all men, took place:

We were at the roast when one of the prince's servants came in with the Jew I had beaten. The poor man came up humbly to me, and spoke as follows:

"I am ordered to come here, sir, to apologize for suspecting the authenticity of the bill of exchange you gave me. I have been punished by being fined the amount of my commission."

"I wish that had been your only punishment," said I.

He made me a profound bow, and went out, saying that I was only too good.

When I 'got back to the inn, I found a letter from Redegonde in which she reproached me tenderly for not having been once to see her all the time I had been at Brunswick, and begging me to breakfast with her in a little country house.

"I shall not be in my mother's company," she added, "but in that of a young lady of your acquaintance, whom, I am sure, you will be glad to see once more."

I liked Redegonde, and I had only neglected her at Brunswick because my means did not allow my making her a handsome present. I resolved to accept her invitation, my curiosity being rather stimulated by the account of the young lady.

I was exact at the time indicated, and I found Redegonde looking charming in a pretty room on the ground floor, and with her was a young artiste whom I had known as a child shortly before I had been put under the Leads. I pretended to be delighted to see her, but I was really quite taken up with Redegonde, and congratulated her upon her pretty house. She said she had taken it for six months, but did not sleep there. After coffee had been served we were on the point of going out for a stroll, when who should come in but the prince. He smiled pleasantly when he saw us, and apologized to Redegonde for interrupting our little party.

The appearance of the prince enlightened me as to the position of my delightful fellow countrywoman, and I understood why she had been so precise about the time at which I was to come. Redegonde had made the conquest of the worthy prince, who was always disposed to gallantry, but felt it his duty during the first year of his marriage with the King of England's sister to preserve some kind of incognito in his amours.

We spent an hour in walking up and down and talking of London and Berlin, but nothing was said of the Jew or the bill of exchange. He was delighted with my warm eulogium of his library at Wolfenbuttel, and laughed with all his heart when I said that unless it had been for the intellectual nourishment I enjoyed, the bad fare at the inn would certainly have reduced me to half my present size.

After bidding a graceful farewell to the nymph, the prince left us, and we heard him galloping away on his horse.

When I was alone with Redegonde, far from begging for new favours, I advised her to be faithful to the prince; but though appearances were certainly not deceitful in this case, she would not admit anything. This was in accordance with her part as young mistress, and I did not reproach her for her want of confidence.

I spent the rest of the day at the inn, and started the next morning at day-break.

When I got to Magdeburg, I took a letter of introduction from General Bekw—— to an officer. He shewed me the fortress, and kept me for three days making me taste all the pleasures of the table, women, and gaming. However, I was very moderate, and managed to increase my savings in a small degree, contenting myself with modest wagers.

From Magdeburg I went straight to Berlin, without caring to stop at Potsdam, as the king was not there. The fearful Prussian roads with their sandy soil made me take three days to do eighteen Prussian miles. Prussia is a country of which much could be made with labour and capital, but I do not think it will ever become a really fine country.

I put up at the "Hotel de Paris," which was both comfortable and economical. Madame Rufin who kept it had entered into the spirit of her business without losing her French politeness, and thus the inn had got a reputation. As soon as I was in my room she came to ask me if I were satisfied, and to make divers arrangements for my comfort. There was a table d'hote, and those who ate in their private rooms paid double.

"This arrangement," I said, "may suit you, but for the present it will not suit me. I want to dine in my own room, but I don't want to pay double; I will therefore pay as if I were in the public room, but if you like you need only send me up half the number of dishes."

"I agree, on the condition that you sup with me; we will not put it in the accounts, and you will only meet friends at my little suppers."

I thought her proposal so curious a one that I had a great inclination to laugh, but finding it at the same time very advantageous I accepted frankly, and as if we had long been friends.

On the first day I was tired, and did not sup with her till the day following. Madame Rufin had a husband who attended to the cooking, and a son, but neither of them came to these suppers. The first time I went to one of them I met an elderly but agreeable and sensible gentleman. He lodged in a room adjoining mine, and called himself Baron Treidel; his sister had married the Duke of Courland, Jean Ernest Biron, or Birlen. The baron, who was extremely pleasant, became my friend, and remained so for the couple of months I spent in Berlin. I also met a Hamburg merchant, named Greve, and his wife, whom he had just married and had brought to Berlin that she might see the marvels of the Warrior-King's Court. She was as pleasant as her husband, and I paid her an assiduous court. A lively and high-spirited individual called Noel, who was the sole and beloved cook of his Prussian Majesty, was the fourth person. He only came rarely to the suppers on account of his duties in the king's kitchen. As I have said, his majesty had only this one cook, and Noel had only one scullion to help him.

M. Noel, the ambassador of the French Republic at the Hague, is, as I am assured, the son of this cook, who was an excellent man.

And here I must say, in despite of my hatred for the French Revolutionary Government, that I am not at all ill pleased that a man of talents should be enabled to fill exalted offices, which under the old system of privilege were often occupied by fools.

If it had not been for the culinary skill of Noel the cook, the famous Atheist physician Lametrie would not have died of indigestion, for the pie he succeeded in eating in his extremity was made by Noel.

Lametrie often supped with Madame Rufin and I thought it disobliging of him to die so soon, for I should have liked to know him, as he was a learned man and full of mirth. He expired laughing, though it is said that death from indigestion is the most painful of all. Voltaire told me that he thought Lametrie the most obstinate Atheist in the world, and I could easily believe it after reading his works. The King of Prussia himself pronounced his funeral oration, using the words, "It is not wonderful that he only believed in the existence of matter, for all the spirit in the world was enclosed in his own body. No one but a king would venture on such a sally in a funeral oration. However, Frederick the Great was a Deist and not an Atheist; but that is of little consequence, since he never allowed the belief in a God to influence his actions in the slightest degree. Some say that an Atheist who ponders over the possible existence of a God is better than a Deist who never thinks of the Deity, but I will not venture to decide this point."

The first visit I paid in Berlin was to Calsabigi, the younger brother of the Calsabigi with whom I had founded the lottery in

Paris in 1757. He had left Paris and his wife too, and had set up a lottery in Brussels; but his extravagance was so great that he became a bankrupt in spite of the efforts of Count Cobenzl to keep him going. He fled from Brussels to Berlin, and was introduced to the King of Prussia. He was a plausible speaker, and persuaded the monarch to establish a lottery, to make him the manager, and to give him the title of Counsellor of State. He promised that the lottery should bring in an annual revenue of at least two hundred thousand crowns, and only asked a percentage of ten per cent. for himself.

The lottery had been going for two years, and had had a great success, as hitherto it had had no large losses; but the king, who knew that the luck might turn, was always in a fidget about it. With this idea he told Calsabigi that he must carry it on on his own responsibility and pay him a hundred thousand crowns per annum, that being the cost of his Italian Theatre.

I happened to call on Calsabigi on the very day on which the king intimated to him this decision. After talking over our old relationship and the vicissitudes we had both experienced, he told me what had happened; it seemed an unexpected blow to him. The next drawing, he said, would be at the king's risk; but the public would have to be informed that in future the lottery would be a private one. He wanted capital to the amount of two million crowns, for he foresaw that otherwise the lottery would collapse, as people would not risk their money without the certainty of being paid in the event of their winning. He said he would guarantee me an income of ten thousand crowns per annum if I succeeded in making the king change his mind, and by way of encouragement he recalled to my mind the effect of my persuasive powers at Paris seven years before.

"'Tis a good omen," said he, "and without any superstition I believe that the good genius of the lottery has brought me to Berlin just now."

I laughed at his illusions, but I pitied him. I shewed him the impossibility of convincing an individual whose only argument was, "I am afraid, and I don't wish to be afraid any longer." He begged me to stay to dinner and introduced me to his wife. This was a double surprise for me, in the first place because I thought General La Motte, as his first wife was called, to be still living, and in the second place because I recognized in this second wife of his, Mdlle. Belanger. I addressed the usual compliments to her and enquired after her mother. She replied with a profound sigh, and told me not to ask any questions about her family as she had only bad news to tell me.

I had known Madame Belanger at Paris; she was a widow with one daughter, and seemed to be well off. Now I saw this daughter, pretty enough and well married, and yet in this doleful humour, and I felt embarrassed and yet curious.

After Calsabigi had placed me in a position to entertain a high opinion of the skill of his cook, he shewed me his horses and carriages, begging me to take a drive with his wife and come back to supper, which, as he said, was his best meal.

When we were in the carriage together, the necessity of talking about something led me to ask the lady by what happy chain of circumstances she found herself the wife of Calsabigi.

"His real wife is still alive, so I have not the misfortune of occupying that position, but everyone in Berlin thinks I am his lawful wife. Three years ago I was deprived of my mother and the means of livelihood at one stroke, for my mother had an annuity. None of my relations were rich enough to help me, and wishing to live virtuously above all things I subsisted for two years on the sale of my mother's furniture, boarding with a worthy woman who made her living by embroidery. I learnt her art, and only went out to mass on Sundays. I was a prey to melancholy, and when I had spent all I had I went to M. Brea, a Genoese, on whom I thought I could rely. I begged him to get me a place as a mere waiting-maid, thinking that I was tolerably competent for such a position. He promised to do what he could for me, and five or six days afterwards he made me the following proposal:

"He read me a letter from Calsabigi, of whom I had never heard, in which he charged him to send a virtuous young lady to Berlin. She must be of good birth, good education, and pleasant appearance, as when his aged and infirm wife died he intended to marry her.

"As such a person would most probably be badly off, Calsabigi begged M. Brea to give her fifty Louis to buy clothes and linen and fifty Louis to journey to Berlin with a maid. M. Brea was also authorized to promise that the young lady should hold the position of Calsabigi's wife, and be presented in that character to all his friends; that she should have a waiting-maid, a carriage, an allowance of clothes, and a certain monthly amount as pin-money to be spent as she chose. He promised, if the arrangement was not found suitable, to set her free at the end of a year, giving her a hundred Louis, and leaving her in possession of whatever money she might have saved, and such clothes and jewels as he might have given her; in fine, if the lady agreed to live with him till he was able to marry her, Calsabigi promised to execute a deed of gift in her favour to the amount of ten thousand crowns which the public would believe to be her dowry, and if he died before being able to marry her she would have a right to claim the aforesaid sum from his estate.

"With such fine promises did Brea persuade me to leave my native country to come and dishonour myself here, for though everybody treats me as if I were his wife, it is probably known that I am only his mistress. I have been here for six months, and I have never had an instant's happiness."

"Has he not kept the conditions you have mentioned?"

"Conditions! Calsabigi's state of health will kill him long before his wife, and in that case I shall have nothing, for he is loaded with debt, and his creditors would have the first claim on the estate. Besides, I do not like him; and the reason is that he loves me too much. You can understand that; his devotion worries me."

"At all events, you can return to Paris in six months' time, or, in fact, do anything you like when the term stipulated has expired.

You will get your hundred louis, and can lay in a pretty stock of linen."

"If I go to Paris I shall be dishonoured, and if I remain here I shall be dishonoured. In fact, I am very unhappy, and Brea is the cause of my woe. Nevertheless, I can't blame him, as he could not have been aware that his friend's property only consisted of debts. And now the king has withdrawn his countenance, the lottery will fail, and Calsabigi will inevitably become a bankrupt."

She had studiously refrained from exaggeration, and I could not help confessing that she was to be pitied. I advised her to try and sell the deed of gift for ten thousand crowns, as it was not likely he would raise any objection.

"I have thought it over," said she, "but to do that I have need of a friend; of course, I do not expect to dispose of it save at a great loss."

I promised to see what I could do for her.

There were four of us at supper. The fourth person was a young man who had helped in the Paris and Brussels Lotteries, and had followed Calsabigi to Berlin. He was evidently in love with Mdlle. Belanger, but I did not think his love was crowned with success.

At dessert Calsabigi begged me to give him my opinion of a scheme he had drafted, the aim of which was to bring in a sum of two million crowns, so that the credit of the lottery might remain secure.

The lady left us to talk business at our ease. She was between twenty-four and twenty-five, and without having much wit she possessed a great knowledge of the usages of society, which is better than wit in a woman; in fine, she had all that a man could well desire. The sentiments I felt for her were confined to those of friendship and esteem after the confidence she had placed in me.

Calsabigi's project was brief, but clear and well imagined. He invited capitalists not to speculate in the lottery, but to guarantee it for a certain sum. In the case of the lottery's losing, each guarantor would have to share in paying according to the sum named, and in like manner they would share in the profits.

I promised to give him my opinion in writing by the next day, and I substituted the following plan for his:

1. A capital of a million, would, I judged, be ample.

2. This million should be divided into a hundred shares of ten thousand crowns each.

3. Each share must be taken up before a notary, who would answer for the shareholder's solvency.

4. All dividends to be paid the third day after the drawing.

5. In case of loss the shareholder to renew his share.

6. A cashier, chosen by a majority of four-fifths of the shareholders, to have the control of all moneys.

7. Winning tickets to be paid the day after the drawing.

8. On the eve of a drawing the shareholders' cashier to have an account of receipts from the lottery cashier, and the former to lock

the safe with three keys, one of which to remain in his hands, one in the hands of the lottery cashier, and one in the hands of the manager of the lottery.

9. Only the simple drawing, the ambe and the terne to be retained; the quarterne and the quine to be abolished.

10. On the three combinations a shilling to be the minimum, and a crown the maximum stake; the offices to be closed twenty-four hours before the drawing.

11. Ten per cent. to go to Calsabigi, the manager; all expenses of farming to be paid by him.

12. Calsabigi to be entitled to the possession of two shares, without a guarantee being required.

I saw by Calsabigi's face that the plan did not please him, but I told him that he would not get shareholders save on these terms, or on terms even less favourable to himself.

He had degraded the lottery to the level of biribi; his luxury and extravagance caused him to be distrusted; it was known that he was head over ears in debt, and the king could not banish the fear that he would be cheated in spite of the keenness of his comptroller-general.

The last drawing under the king's sanction made everyone in good spirits, for the lottery lost twenty thousand crowns. The king sent the money immediately by a privy councillor, but it was said, when he heard the result of the drawing, that he burst out laughing, observing,—

"I knew it would be so, and I am only too happy to have got quit of it so cheaply."

I thought it my duty to go and sup with the director to console him, and I found him in a state of great depression. He could not help thinking that his unhappy drawing would make the task of getting shareholders more difficult than ever. Hitherto the lottery had always been a gainer, but its late loss could not have come at a worse time.

Nevertheless, he did not lose heart, and the next morning the public were informed by printed bills that the office would remain closed till a sufficient number of guarantors were found.

CHAPTER XVIII

Lord Keith—My Appointment to Meet the King in the Garden of Sans-Souci My Conversation with Frederick the Great—Madame Denis The Pomeranian Cadets—Lambert—I Go to Mitau My Welcome at the Court, and My Administrative Journey

The fifth day after my arrival at Berlin I presented myself to the lord-marshal, who since the death of his brother had been styled Lord Keith. I had seen him in London after his return from Scotland, where he had been reinstated in the family estates, which had been confiscated for Jacobinism. Frederick the Great was supposed to have brought this about. Lord Keith lived at Berlin, resting on his laurels, and enjoying the blessings of peace.

With his old simplicity of manner he told me he was glad to see me again, and asked if I proposed making any stay at Berlin. I replied that I would willingly do so if the king would give me a suitable office. I asked him if he would speak a word in my favour; but he replied that the king liked to judge men's characters for himself, and would often discover merit where no one had suspected its presence, and vice versa.

He advised me to intimate to the king in writing that I desired to have the honour of an interview. "When you speak to him," the good old man added, "you may say that you know me, and the king will doubtless address me on the subject, and you may be sure what I say shall not be to your disadvantage."

"But, my lord, how can I write to a monarch of whom I know nothing, and who knows nothing of me? I should not have thought of such a step."

"I daresay, but don't you wish to speak to him?"

"Certainly."

"That is enough. Your letter will make him aware of your desire and nothing more."

"But will he reply?"

"Undoubtedly; he replies to everybody. He will tell you when and where he will see you. His Majesty is now at Sans-Souci. I am curious to know the nature of your interview with the monarch who, as you can see, is not afraid of being imposed on."

When I got home I wrote a plain but respectful letter to the king, asking where and at what time I could introduce myself to him.

In two days I received a letter signed "Frederick," in which the receipt of my letter was acknowledged, and I was told that I should find his majesty in the garden of Sans-Souci at four o'clock.

As may be imagined I was punctual to my appointment. I was at Sans-Souci at three, clad in a simple black dress. When I got into the court-yard there was not so much as a sentinel to stop me, so I went on mounted a stair, and opened a door in front of me. I found myself in a picture-gallery, and the curator came up to me and offered to shew me over it.

"I have not come to admire these masterpieces," I replied, "but to see the king, who informed me in writing that I should find him in the garden."

"He is now at a concert playing the flute; he does so every day after dinner. Did he name any time?"

"Yes, four o'clock, but he will have forgotten that."

"The king never forgets anything; he will keep the appointment, and you will do well to go into the garden and await him."

I had been in the garden for some minutes when I saw him appear, followed by his reader and a pretty spaniel. As soon as he saw me he accosted me, taking off his old hat, and pronouncing my name. Then he asked in a terrible voice what I wanted of him. This greeting surprised me, and my voice stuck in my throat.

"Well, speak out. Are you not the person who wrote to me?"

"Yes, sire, but I have forgotten everything now. I thought that I should not be awed by the majesty of a king, but I was mistaken. My lord-marshal should have warned me."

"Then he knows you? Let us walk. What is it that you want? What do you think of my garden?"

His enquiries after my needs and of his garden were simultaneous. To any other person I should have answered that I did not know anything about gardening, but this would have been equivalent to refusing to answer the question; and no monarch, even if he be a philosopher, could endure that. I therefore replied that I thought the garden superb.

"But," he said, "the gardens of Versailles are much finer."

"Yes, sire, but that is chiefly on account of the fountains."

"True, but it is not my fault; there is no water here. I have spent more than three hundred thousand crowns to get water, but unsuccessfully."

"Three hundred thousand crowns, sire! If your majesty had spent them all at once, the fountains should be here."

"Oh, oh! I see you are acquainted with hydraulics."

I could not say that he was mistaken, for fear of offending him, so I simply bent my head, which might mean either yes or no. Thank God the king did not trouble to test my knowledge of the science of hydraulics, with which I was totally unacquainted.

He kept on the move all the time, and as he turned his head from one side to the other hurriedly asked me what forces Venice could put into the field in war time.

"Twenty men-of-war, sire, and a number of galleys."

"What are the land forces?"

"Seventy thousand men, sire; all of whom are subjects of the Republic, and assessing each village at one man."

"That is not true; no doubt you wish to amuse me by telling me these fables. Give me your opinions on taxation."

This was the first conversation I had ever had with a monarch. I made a rapid review of the situation, and found myself much in the same position as an actor of the improvised comedy of the Italians, who is greeted by the hisses of the gods if he stops short a moment. I therefore replied with all the airs of a doctor of finance that I could say something about the theory of taxation.

"That's what I want," he replied, "for the practice is no business of yours."

"There are three kinds of taxes, considered as to their effects. The first is ruinous, the second a necessary evil, and the third invariably beneficial."

"Good! Go on."

"The ruinous impost is the royal tax, the necessary is the military, and the beneficial is the popular."

As I had not given the subject any thought I was in a disagreeable position, for I was obliged to go on speaking, and yet not to talk nonsense.

"The royal tax, sire, is that which deplenishes the purses of the subject to fill the coffers of the king."

"And that kind of tax is always ruinous, you think."

"Always, sire; it prevents the circulation of money—the soul of commerce and the mainstay of the state."

"But if the tax be levied to keep up the strength of the army, you say it is a necessary evil."

"Yes, it is necessary and yet evil, for war is an evil."

"Quite so; and now about the popular tax."

"This is always a benefit, for the monarch takes with one hand and gives with the other; he improves towns and roads, founds schools, protects the sciences, cherishes the arts; in fine, he directs this tax towards improving the condition and increasing the happiness of his people."

"There is a good deal of truth in that. I suppose you know Calsabigi?"

"I ought to, your majesty, as he and I established the Genoa Lottery   at
Paris seven years ago."

"In what class would you put this taxation, for you will agree that it is taxation of a kind?"

"Certainly, sire, and not the least important. It is beneficial when the monarch spends his profits for the good of the people."

"But the monarch may lose?"

"Once in fifty."

"Is that conclusion the result of a mathematical calculation?"

"Yes, sire."

"Such calculations often prove deceptive."

"Not so, may it please your majesty, when God remains neutral."

"What has God got to do with it?"

"Well, sire, we will call it destiny or chance."

"Good! I may possibly be of your opinion as to the calculation, but I don't like your Genoese Lottery. It seems to me an elaborate swindle, and I would have nothing more to do with it, even if it were positively certain that I should never lose."

"Your majesty is right, for the confidence which makes the people risk their money in a lottery is perfectly fallacious."

This was the end of our strange dialogue, and stopping before a building he looked me over, and then, after a short silence, observed,—

"Do you know that you are a fine man?"

"Is it possible that, after the scientific conversation we have had, your majesty should select the least of the qualities which adorn your life guardsmen for remark?"

The king smiled kindly, and said,—

"As you know Marshal Keith, I will speak to him of you."

With that he took off his hat, and bade me farewell. I retired with a profound bow.

Three or four days after the marshal gave me the agreeable news that I had found favour in the king's eyes, and that his majesty thought of employing me.

I was curious to learn the nature of this employment, and being in no kind of hurry I resolved to await events in Berlin. The time passed pleasantly enough, for I was either with Calsabigi, Baron Treidel, or my landlady, and when these resources failed me, I used to walk in the park, musing over the events of my life.

Calsabigi had no difficulty in obtaining permission to continue the lottery on his own account, and he boldly announced that henceforward he would conduct the lottery on his own risk. His audacity was crowned with success, and he obtained a profit of a hundred thousand crowns. With this he paid most of his debts, and gave his mistress ten thousand crowns, she returning the document entitling her to that amount. After this lucky drawing it was easy to find guarantors, and the lottery went on successfully for two or three years.

Nevertheless Calsabigi ended by becoming bankrupt and died poor enough in Italy. He might be compared to the Danaides; the more he got the more he spent. His mistress eventually made a respectable marriage and returned to Paris, where she lived in comfort.

At the period of which I am speaking, the Duchess of Brunswick, the king's sister, came to pay him a visit. She was accompanied by her daughter who married the Crown Prince of Prussia in the following year. I saw the king in a suit of lustring trimmed with gold lace, and black silk stockings on his legs. He looked truly comic, and more like a theatrical heavy father than a great king. He came into the hall with his sister on his arm and attracted universal attention, for only very old men could remember seeing him without his uniform and top-boots.

I was not aware that the famous Madame Denis was at Berlin, and it was therefore an agreeable surprise to me to see her in the ballet one evening, dancing a pas seul in an exquisite manner. We were old friends, and I resolved to pay her a visit the next day.

I must tell the reader (supposing I ever have one), that when I was about twelve years old I went to the theatre with my mother and saw, not without much heart-beating, a girl of eight who danced a minuet in so ravishing a manner that the whole house applauded loudly. This young dancer, who was the pantaloon's daughter, charmed me to such a degree that I could not resist going to her dressing-room to compliment her on her performance. I wore the cassock in those days, and she was astonished when she heard her father order her to get up and kiss me. She kissed me, nevertheless, with much grace, and though I received the compliment with a good deal of awkwardness I was so delighted, that I could not help buying her a little ring from a toy merchant in the theatre. She kissed me again with great gratitude and enthusiasm.

The pleasantest part about this was that the sequin I had given for the ring belonged to Dr. Gozzi, and so when I went back to him I was in a pitiable state, for I had not only spent money which did not belong to me, but I had spent it for so small a favour as a kiss.

I knew that the next day I should have to give an account of the money he had entrusted to me, and not having the least idea as to what I should say, I had a bad night of it. The next morning everything came out, and my mother made up the sequin to the doctor. I laugh now when I think of this childish piece of gallantry, which was an omen of the extent to which my heart was to be swayed by the fair sex.

The toy-woman who had sold me the ring came the next day at dinner-time to our house, and after producing several rings and trinkets which were judged too dear, she began to praise my generosity, and said that I had not thought the ring I had given to pretty Jeannette too dear. This did my business; and I had to confess the whole, laying my fault to the account of love, and promising not to do such a thing again. But when I uttered the word love, everybody roared with laughter, and began to make cruel game of me. I wished myself a mile away, and registered an interior resolve never to confess my faults again. The reader knows how well I kept my promise.

The pantaloon's little daughter was my mother's goddaughter, and my thoughts were full of her. My mother, who loved me and saw my pain, asked me if I would like the little girl to be asked to supper. My grandmother, however, opposed the idea, and I was obliged to her.

The day after this burlesque scene I returned to Padua, where Bettina soon made me forget the little ballet-girl. I saw her again at Charlottenbourg, and that was now seventeen years ago.

I longed to have a talk with her, and to see whether she would remember me, though I did not expect her to do so. I asked if her husband Denis was with her, and they told me that the king had banished him because he ill-treated her.

I called on her the day after the performance, and was politely received, but she said she did not think she had had the pleasure of seeing me before.

By degrees I told her of the events of her childhood, and how she enchanted all Venice by the grace with which she danced the minuet. She interrupted me by saying that at that time she was only six years old.

"You could not be more," I replied, "for I was only ten; and nevertheless, I fell in love with you, and never have I forgotten the kiss you gave me by your father's order in return for some trifling present I made you."

"Be quiet; you gave me a beautiful ring, and I kissed you of my own free will. You wore the cassock then. I have never forgotten you. But can it really be you?"

"It is indeed."

"I am delighted to see you again. But I could never have recognized you, and I suppose you would not have recognized me."

"No, I should not have known you, unless I had heard your name mentioned."

"One alters in twenty years, you know."

"Yes, one cannot expect to have the same face as at six."

"You can bear witness that I am not more than twenty-six, though some evil speakers give me ten years more."

"You should not take any notice of such calumnies, my dear. You are in the flower of your age, and made for the service of love. For my part, I congratulate myself on being able to tell you that you are the first woman that inspired me with a real passion."

We could not help becoming affectionate if we continued to keep up the conversation in this style, but experience had taught us that it was well to remain as we were for the present.

Madame Denis was still fresh and youthful looking, though she persisted in abbreviating her age by ten years. Of course she could not deceive me, and she must have known it, nevertheless, she liked me to bear outward testimony to her youthfulness. She would have detested me if I had attempted to prove to her what she knew perfectly well, but did not care to confess. No doubt she cared little for my thoughts on the subject, and she may have imagined that I owed her gratitude for diminishing her age, as it enabled me to diminish my own to make our tales agree. However, I did not trouble myself much about it, for it is almost a duty in an actress to disguise her age, as in spite of talent the public will not forgive a woman for having been born too soon.

I thought her behaviour augured well, and I hoped she would not make me languish long. She shewed me her house, which was all elegance and good taste. I asked her if she had a lover, and she replied with a smile that all Berlin thought so, but that it was nevertheless deceived on the principal point, as the individual in question was more of a father than a lover.

"But you deserve to have a real lover; I cannot conceive how you can do without one."

"I assure you I don't trouble myself about it. I am subject to convulsions, which are the plague of my life. I want to try the Teplitz waters, which are said to be excellent for all nervous affections; but the king has refused his permission, which I, nevertheless, hope to obtain next year."

I felt ardently disposed, and I thought she was pleased with the restraint I put upon myself.

"Will you be annoyed," said I, "if I call upon you frequently?"

"If you don't mind I will call myself your niece, or your cousin, and then we can see each other."

"Do you know that that may possibly be true? I would not swear that you were not my sister."

This sally made us talk of the friendship that had subsisted between her father and my mother, and we allowed ourselves those caresses which are permitted to near relations; but feeling that things were going too far we ceased. As she bade me farewell, she asked me to dine with her the next day, and I accepted.

As I went back to my inn I reflected on the strange combinations which made my life one continuous chain of events, and I felt it my duty to give thanks to eternal Providence, for I felt that I had been born under a happy star.

The next day, when I went to dine with Madame Denis, I found a numerous company assembled. The first person who greeted me with the warmth of an old friend was a young dancer named Aubri, whom I had known at Paris and at Venice. He was famous for having been the lover of one of the most exalted Venetian ladies, and at the same time her husband's pathic. It was said that this scandalous intimacy was of such a nature that Aubri used to sleep between the husband and wife. At the beginning of Lent the State Inquisitors sent him to Trieste. He introduced me to his wife, who danced like himself and was called La Panting. He had married her at St. Petersburg, from which city he had just come, and they were going to spend the winter in Paris. The next person who advanced to greet me was a fat man, who held out his hand and said we had been friends twenty-five years ago, but that we were so young then that it would be no wonder if we did not know each other. "We knew each other at Padua, at Dr. Gozzi's," he added; "my name is Joseph da Loglio."

"I remember you," I replied, "in those days you were violoncello at the
Russian chapel."

"Exactly; and now I am returning to my native land to leave it no more. I have the honour to introduce you to my wife, who was born at St. Petersburg, but is a daughter of Modonis the violinist,

123

whose reputation is European. In a week I shall be at Dresden, where I hope to have the honour of seeing Madame Casanova, your mother."

I was delighted to find myself in such congenial society, but I could see that Madame Denis did not relish these recollections extending over a quarter of a century, and I turned the conversation to the events at St. Petersburg which had resulted in Catherine the Great ascending the throne. Da Loglio told us that he had taken a small part in this conspiracy, and had thought it prudent to get out of the way. "Fortunately," he added, "this was a contingency I had long provided against, and I am in a position to spend the rest of my days in comfort in Italy."

Madame Denis then observed:

"A week ago a Piedmontese, named Audar, was introduced to me. He had been a chief mover in the conspiracy, and the empress gave him a present of a hundred thousand roubles and an order to leave Russia immediately."

I heard afterwards that this Audar bought an estate in Piedmont on which he built a fine mansion. In two or three years it was struck by a thunder-bolt, and the unfortunate man was killed in the ruins of his own house. If this was a blow from an Almighty hand, it could not, at all events, have been directed by the genius of Russia, for if the unfortunate Peter III. had lived, he would have retarded Russian civilization by a hundred years.

The Empress Catherine rewarded all the foreigners who had assisted her in her plots most magnificently, and shewed herself grateful to the Russians who had helped her to mount the throne; while, like a crafty politician, she sent such nobles as she suspected to be averse to revolution out of the country.

It was Da Loglio and his pretty wife who determined me to betake myself to Russia in case the King of Prussia did not give me any employment. I was assured that I should make my fortune there, and Da Loglio promised to give me good instructions.

As soon as this worthy man left Berlin my intimacy with Madame Denis commenced. One night when I was supping with her she was seized with convulsions which lasted all the night. I did not leave her for a moment, and in the morning, feeling quite recovered, her gratitude finished what my love had begun twenty-six years before, and our amorous commerce lasted while I stayed at Berlin. We shall hear of her again at Florence six years later.

Some days after Madame Denis took me to Potsdam to shew me all the sights of the town. Our intimacy offended no one, for she was generally believed to be my niece, and the general who kept her either believed the report, or like a man of sense pretended to believe it.

Amongst other notable things I saw at Potsdam was the sight of the king commanding the first battalion of his grenadiers, all picked men, the flower of the Prussian army.

The room which we occupied at the inn faced a walk by which the king passed when he came from the castle. The shutters were all closed, and our landlady told us that on one occasion when a pretty dancer called La Reggiana was sleeping in the same room, the king had seen her in 'puris naturalibus'. This was too much for his modesty, and he had ordered the shutters to be closed, and closed they had remained, though this event was four years old. The king had some cause to fear, for he had been severely treated by La Barbarina. In the king's bedroom we saw her portrait, that of La Cochois, sister to the actress who became Marchioness d'Argens, and that of Marie Theresa, with whom Frederick had been in love, or rather he had been in love with the idea of becoming emperor.

After we had admired the beauty and elegance of the castle, we could not help admiring the way in which the master of the castle was lodged. He had a mean room, and slept on a little bed with a screen around it. There was no dressing-gown and no slippers. The valet shewed us an old cap which the king put on when he had a cold; it looked as if it must be very uncomfortable. His majesty's bureau was a table covered with pens, paper, half-burnt manuscripts, and an ink-pot; beside it was a sofa. The valet told us that these manuscripts contained the history of the last Prussian war, and the king had been so annoyed by their accidentally getting burnt that he had resolved to have no more to do with the work. He probably changed his mind, for the book, which is little esteemed, was published shortly after his death.

Five or six weeks after my curious conversation with the monarch, Marshal Keith told me that his majesty had been pleased to create me a tutor to the new corps of Pomeranian cadets which he was just establishing. There were to be fifteen cadets and five tutors, so that each should have the care of three pupils. The salary was six hundred crowns and board found. The duty of the tutors was to follow or accompany the cadets wherever they went, Court included. I had to be quick in making up my mind, for the four others were already installed, and his majesty did not like to be kept waiting. I asked Lord Keith where the college was, and I promised to give him a reply by the next day.

I had to summon all my powers of self-restraint to my assistance when I heard this extravagant proposal as coming from a man who was so discreet in most things, but my astonishment was increased when I saw the abode of these fifteen young noblemen of rich Pomerania. It consisted of three or four great rooms almost devoid of furniture, several whitewashed bedrooms, containing a wretched bed, a deal table, and two deal chairs. The young cadets, boys of twelve or thirteen, all looked dirty and untidy, and were boxed up in a wretched uniform which matched admirably their rude and rustic faces. They were in company with their four governors, whom I took for their servants, and who looked at me in a stupefied manner, not daring to think that I was to be their future colleague.

Just as I was going to bid an eternal farewell to this abode of misery, one of the governors put his head out of the window and exclaimed,—

"The king is riding up."

I could not avoid meeting him, and besides, I was glad enough to see him again, especially in such a place.

His majesty came up with his friend Icilius, examined everything, and saw me, but did not honour me with a word. I was elegantly dressed, and wore my cross set with brilliants. But I had to bite my lips so as not to burst out laughing when Frederick the Great got in a towering rage at a chamber utensil which stood beside one of the beds, and which did not appear to be in a very cleanly condition.

"Whose bed is this?" cried the monarch.

"Mine, sire," answered a trembling cadet.

"Good! but it is not you I am angry with; where is your governor?"

The fortunate governor presented himself, and the monarch, after honouring him with the title of blockhead, proceeded to scold him roundly. However, he ended by saying that there was a servant, and that the governor ought to see that he did his work properly. This disgusting scene was enough for me, and I hastened to call on Marshal Keith to announce my determination. The old soldier laughed at the description I gave him of the academy, and said I was quite right to despise such an office; but that I ought, nevertheless, to go and thank the king before I left Berlin. I said I did not feel inclined for another interview with such a man, and he agreed to present my thanks and excuses in my stead.

I made up my mind to go to Russia, and began my preparations in good earnest. Baron Treidel supported my resolve by offering to give me a letter of introduction to his sister, the Duchess of Courland. I wrote to M. de Bragadin to 'give me a letter for a banker at St. Petersburg, and to remit me through him every month a sum which would keep me in comfort.

I could not travel without a servant, and chance kindly provided me with one. I was sitting with Madame Rufin, when a young Lorrainer came in; like Bias, he bore all his fortune with him, but, in his case, it was carried under his arm. He introduced himself thus:

"Madam, my name is Lambert, I come from Lorraine, and I wish to lodge here."

"Very good, sir, but you must pay for your board and lodging every day."

"That, madam, is out of the question, for I have not got a farthing, but
I shall have some money when I discover who I am."

"I am afraid I cannot put you up on those conditions, sir."

He was going away with a mortified air, when my heart was touched, and I called him back.

"Stay," said I, "I will pay for you to-day."

Happiness beamed over his face.

"What have you got in that little bundle?" said I.

"Two shirts, a score of mathematical books, and some other trifles."

I took him to my room, and finding him tolerably well educated, I asked him how he came to be in such a state of destitution.

"I come from Strasburg," he replied, "and a cadet of a regiment stationed there having given me a blow in a coffee-house I paid him a visit the next day in his own room and stabbed him there.

"After this I went home, made up my bundle, and left the town. I walked all the way and lived soberly, so that my money lasted till this morning. To-morrow I shall write to my mother, who lives at Luneville, and I am sure she will send me some money."

"And what do you think of doing?"

"I want to become a military engineer, but if needs must I am ready to enlist as a private soldier."

"I can give you board and lodging till you hear from your mother."

"Heaven has sent you in my way," said he, kissing my hand gratefully.

I did not suspect him of deceiving me, though he stumbled somewhat in his narrative. However my curiosity led me to write to M. Schauenbourg, who was then at Strasburg, to enquire if the tale were true.

The next day I happened to meet an officer of engineers, who told me that young men of education were so plentiful that they did not receive them into the service unless they were willing to serve as common soldiers. I was sorry for the young man to be reduced so low as that. I began to spend some time with him every day in mathematical calculations, and I conceived the idea of taking him with me to St. Petersburg, and broached the subject to him.

"It would be a piece of good fortune for me," he replied, "and to shew my gratitude I will gladly wait on you as a servant during the journey."

He spoke French badly, but as he was a Lorrainer I was not astonished at that. Nevertheless I was surprised to find that he did not know a word of Latin, and that his spelling was of the wildest description. He saw me laughing, but did not seem in the least ashamed. Indeed he said that he had only gone to school to learn mathematics, and that he was very glad that he had escaped the infliction of learning grammar. Indeed, on every subject besides mathematics, he was profoundly ignorant. He had no manners whatever; in fact, he was a mere peasant.

Ten or twelve days later I received a letter from M. de Schauenbourg, saying that the name of Lambert was unknown in Strasburg, and that no cadet had been killed or wounded.

When I shewed Lambert this letter he said that as he wished to enter the army he thought it would be of service to him to shew that he was brave, adding that as this lie had not been told with the idea of imposing on me I should forgive it.

"Poverty," said he, "is a rascally teacher, that gives a man some bad lessons. I am not a liar by disposition, but I have nevertheless told you a lie on another and a more important matter. I don't expect any money whatever from my poor mother, who rather needs that I should send money to her. So forgive me, and be sure I shall be a faithful servant to you."

I was always ready to forgive other men's peccadilloes, and not without cause. I liked Lambert's line of argument, and told him that we would set out in five or six days.

Baron Bodisson, a Venetian who wanted to sell the king a picture by Andrea del Sarto, asked me to come with him to Potsdam and the desire of seeing the monarch once again made me accept the invitation. When I reached Potsdam I went to see the parade at which Frederick was nearly always to be found. When he saw me he came up and asked me in a familiar manner when I was going to start for St. Petersburg.

"In five or six days, if your majesty has no objection."

"I wish you a pleasant journey; but what do you hope to do in that land?"

"What I hoped to do in this land, namely, to please the sovereign."

"Have you got an introduction to the empress?"

"No, but I have an introduction to a banker."

"Ah! that's much better. If you pass through Prussia on your return I shall be delighted to hear of your adventures in Russia."

"Farewell, sire."

Such was the second interview I had with this great king, whom I never saw again.

After I had taken leave of all my friends I applied to Baron Treidel, who gave me a letter for M. de Kaiserling, lord-chancellor at

Mitau, and another letter for his sister, the Duchess of Courland, and I spent the last night with the charming Madame Denis. She bought my post-chaise, and I started with two hundred ducats in my purse. This would have been ample for the whole journey if I had not been so foolish as to reduce it by half at a party of pleasure with some young merchants at Dantzic. I was thus unable to stay a few days at Koenigsberg, though I had a letter to Field-Marshal von Lewald, who was the governor of the place. I could only stay one day to dine with this pleasant old soldier, who gave me a letter for his friend General Woiakoff, the Governor of Riga.

I found I was rich enough to arrive at Mitau in state, and I therefore took a carriage and six, and reached my destination in three days. At the inn where I put up I found a Florentine artiste named Bregonci, who overwhelmed me with caresses, telling me that I had loved her when I was a boy and wore the cassock. I saw her six years later at Florence, where she was living with Madame Denis.

The day after my departure from Memel, I was accosted in the open country by a man whom I recognized as a Jew. He informed me that I was on Polish territory, and that I must pay duty on whatever merchandise I had with me.

"I am no merchant," said I, "and you will get nothing out of me."

"I have the right to examine your effects," replied the Israelite, "and I mean to make use of it."

"You are a madman," I exclaimed, and I ordered the postillion to whip him off.

But the Jew ran and seized the fore horses by the bridle and stopped us, and the postillion, instead of whipping him, waited with Teutonic calm for me to come and send the Jew away. I was in a furious rage, and leaping out with my cane in one hand and a pistol in the other I soon put the Jew to flight after applying about a dozen good sound blows to his back. I noticed that during the combat my fellow-traveller, my Archimedes-in-ordinary, who had been asleep all the way, did not offer to stir. I reproached him for his cowardice; but he told me that he did not want the Jew to say that we had set on him two to one.

I arrived at Mitau two days after this burlesque adventure and got down at the inn facing the castle. I had only three ducats left.

The next morning I called on M. de Kaiserling, who read the Baron de Treidel's letter, and introduced me to his wife, and left me with her to take the baron's letter to his sister.

Madame de Kaiserling ordered a cup of chocolate to be brought me by a beautiful young Polish girl, who stood before me with lowered eyes as if she wished to give me the opportunity of examining her at ease. As I looked at her a whim came into my head, and, as the reader is aware, I have never resisted any of my whims. However, this was a curious one. As I have said, I had only three ducats left, but after I had emptied the cup of chocolate I put it back on the plate and the three ducats with it.

The chancellor came back and told me that the duchess could not see me just then, but that she invited me to a supper and ball she was giving that evening. I accepted the supper and refused the ball, on the pretext that I had only summer clothes and a black suit. It was in the beginning of October, and the cold was already commencing to make itself felt. The chancellor returned to the Court, and I to my inn.

Half an hour later a chamberlain came to bring me her highness's compliments, and to inform me that the ball would be a masked one, and that I could appear in domino.

"You can easily get one from the Jews," he added. He further informed me that the ball was to have been a full-dress one, but that the duchess had sent word to all the guests that it would be masked, as a stranger who was to be present had sent on his trunks.

"I am sorry to have caused so much trouble," said I.

"Not at all," he replied, "the masked ball will be much more relished by the people."

He mentioned the time it was to begin, and left me.

No doubt the reader will think that I found myself in an awkward predicament, and I will be honest and confess I was far from being at my ease. However, my good luck came to my assistance.

As Prussian money (which is the worst in Germany) is not current in Russia, a Jew came and asked me if I had any friedrichs d'or, offering to exchange them against ducats without putting me to any loss.

"I have only ducats," I replied, "and therefore I cannot profit by your offer."

"I know it sir, and you give them away very cheaply."

Not understanding what he meant, I simply gazed at him, and he went on to say that he would be glad to let me have two hundred ducats if I would kindly give him a bill on St. Petersburg for roubles to that amount.

I was somewhat surprised at the fellow's trustfulness, but after pretending to think the matter over I said that I was not in want of ducats, but that I would take a hundred to oblige him. He counted out the money gratefully, and I gave him a bill on the banker, Demetrio Papanelopoulo, for whom Da Loglio had given me a letter. The Jew went his way, thanking me, and saying that he would send me some beautiful dominos to choose from. Just then I remembered that I wanted silk stockings, and I sent Lambert after the Jew to tell him to send some. When he came back he told me that the landlord had stopped him to say that I scattered my ducats broadcast, as the Jew had informed him that I had given three ducats to Madame de Kaiserling's maid.

This, then, was the key to the mystery, and it made me lose myself in wonder at the strangeness of the decrees of fortune. I should not have been able to get a single crown at Mitau if it had not been for the way in which I scattered my three remaining ducats. No doubt the astonished girl had published my generosity all over the town, and the Jew, intent on money-making, had hastened to offer his ducats to the rich nobleman who thought so little of his money.

I repaired to Court at the time appointed, and M. de Kaiserling immediately presented me to the duchess, and she to the duke, who was the celebrated Biron, or Birlen, the former favourite of Anna Ivanovna. He was six feet in height, and still preserved some traces of having been a fine man, but old age had laid its heavy hand on him. I had a long talk with him the day after the ball.

A quarter of an hour after my arrival, the ball began with a polonaise. I was a stranger with introductions, so the duchess asked me to open the ball with her. I did not know the dance, but I managed to acquit myself honourably in it, as the steps are simple and lend themselves to the fancy of the dancer.

After the polonaise we danced minuets, and a somewhat elderly lady asked me if I could dance the "King Conqueror," so I proceeded to execute it with her. It had gone out of fashion since the time of the Regency, but my companion may have shone in it in those days. All the younger ladies stood round and watched us with admiration.

After a square dance, in which I had as partner Mdlle. de Manteufel, the prettiest of the duchess's maids of honour, her highness told me that supper was ready. I came up to her and offered my arm, and presently found myself seated beside her at a table laid for twelve where I was the only gentleman. However, the reader need not envy me; the ladies were all elderly dowagers, who had long lost the power of turning men's heads. The duchess took the greatest care of my comforts, and at the end of the repast gave me with her own hands a glass of liqueur, which I took for Tokay and praised accordingly, but it turned out to be only old English ale. I took her back to the ball when we rose from table. The young chamberlain who had invited me told me the names of all the ladies present, but I had no time to pay my court to any of them.

The next day I dined with M. de Kaiserling, and handed Lambert over to a Jew to be clothed properly.

The day after I dined with the duke with a party consisting only of men. The old prince made me do most of the talking, and towards the end of the dinner the conversation fell upon the resources of the country which was rich in minerals and semi-minerals. I took it into my head to say that these resources ought to be developed, and that they would become precious if that were done. To justify this remark I had to speak upon the matter as if I had made it my principal study. An old chamberlain, who had the control of the mines, after allowing me to exhaust my enthusiasm, began to discuss the question himself, made divers objections, but seemed to approve of many of my remarks.

If I had reflected when I began to speak in this manner that I should have to act up to my words, I should certainly have said much less; but as it was, the duke fancied that I knew much more than I cared to say. The result was that, when the company had risen from the table, he asked me if I could spare him a fortnight on my way to St. Petersburg. I said I should be glad to oblige him, and he took me to his closet and said that the chamberlain who had spoken to me would conduct me over all the mines and manufactories in his duchies, and that he would be much obliged if I would write down any observations that struck me. I agreed to his proposal, and said I would start the next day.

The duke was delighted with my compliance, and gave the chamberlain the necessary orders, and it was agreed that he should call for me at day-break with a carriage and six.

When I got home I made my preparations, and told Lambert to be ready to accompany me with his case of instruments. I then informed him of the object of the journey, and he promised to assist me to the best of his ability, though he knew nothing about mines, and still less of the science of administration.

We started at day-break, with a servant on the box, and two others preceding us on horseback, armed to the teeth. We changed horses every two or three hours, and the chamberlain having brought plenty of wine we refreshed ourselves now and again.

The tour lasted a fortnight, and we stopped at five iron and copper manufactories. I found it was not necessary to have much technical knowledge to make notes on what I saw; all I required was a little sound argument, especially in the matter of economy, which was the duke's main object. In one place I advised reforms, and in another I counselled the employment of more hands as likely to benefit the revenue. In one mine where thirty convicts were employed I ordered the construction of a short canal, by which three wheels could be turned and twenty men saved. Under my direction Lambert drew the plans, and made the measurements with perfect accuracy. By means of other canals I proposed to drain whole valleys, with a view to obtain the sulphur with which the soil was permeated.

I returned to Mitau quite delighted at having made myself useful, and at having discovered in myself a talent which I had never suspected. I spent the following day in making a fair copy of my report and in having the plans done on a larger scale. The day after I took the whole to the duke, who seemed well pleased; and as I was taking leave of him at the same time he said he would have me drive to Riga in one of his carriages, and he gave me a letter for his son, Prince Charles, who was in garrison there.

The worthy old man told me to say plainly whether I should prefer a jewel or a sum of money of equivalent value.

"From a philosopher like your highness," I replied, "I am not afraid to take money, for it may be more useful to me than jewels."

Without more ado he gave me a draft for four hundred albertsthalers, which I got cashed immediately, the albertsthaler being worth half a ducat. I bade farewell to the duchess, and dined a second time with M. de Kaiserling.

The next day the young chamberlain came to bring me the duke's letter, to wish me a pleasant journey, and to tell me that the Court carriage was at my door. I set out well pleased with the assistance the stuttering Lambert had given me, and by noon I was at Riga. The first thing I did was to deliver my letter of introduction to Prince Charles.

The End

www.ingramcontent.com/pod-product-compliance
Lightning Source LLC
Chambersburg PA
CBHW070034300526
45794CB00001B/489